DOORSTEP TO DAMEHOOD

An Autobiography

BY

KATHARINE M.E. LISTON

Best wishes from Katharine M.E. Liston

Published by Neetah Books

First printing: January 2017
Copyright © 2016 by Katharine Liston.
All rights reserved.

A CIP catalogue for this title is available from the British Library.
ISBN: 978-1-908898-29-6

This book is dedicated
to all my friends
whom I love dearly.

AUTHOR'S NOTE

John Cairney suggested - no, insisted - that I should write this book, and the title just tripped off his tongue. He deserves a word of thanks from me. Sometimes we all need a push and a shove, don't we? What happened - particularly in childhood - was much worse than I have described. There are things I just could not bear to write about. After all, some things are better left unsaid. It has not been easy but, nevertheless, I hope that there will be much of interest within these pages. It is as well to remember, however, that only he who wears the shoe knows where it pinches.

This poem, by A E Housman, sums me up pretty well:

> *The stars have not dealt me the worst they could do;*
> *My pleasures are plenty, my troubles are two.*
> *But, oh, my two troubles, they reave me of rest,*
> *The brains in my head and the heart in my breast.*
>
> *Oh grant me the ease that is granted so free,*
> *The birthright of multitudes, give it to me,*
> *That relish their victuals, and rest on their bed*
> *With flint in the bosom and guts in the head.*

KMEL

CONTENTS

1 - In the Beginning

'...a whole is that which has a beginning, a middle, and an end.'
(Aristotle, *Poetics*)

In the arms of Sister Jinty McPhail.

The year was 1930. The month was November. A new-born baby girl lay on the steps of the famous maternity hospital in Rottenrow, Glasgow. I was that baby girl. Nothing whatsoever was known about me but I was looked after in the hospital by Sister Jinty McPhail and, when well enough, I was adopted into the strangest and most unsuitable household imaginable. Even to this day, I'm not sure exactly how this was brought about, other than it was arranged by the local GP. Fortunately, nothing like that could happen nowadays in such a casual manner.

I was given the names Katharine Margaret Ella and, for some strange reason, the spelling of the name Katharine plagued me for the rest of my life. It was spelt any old how and I frequently got called Kathleen. I often used to wonder if Katharine Hepburn had experienced the same bother.

About ten months or so later, another girl was adopted into this family. She was a foundling abandoned in a close in the Gorbals and there was nothing whatsoever known about her either. For reasons of privacy, I will refer to her by the name Jane.

When I mention my father, mother or sister in this book you must be constantly aware of the fact that I have no blood relations of whom I'm aware, but I have no option but to use these terms to refer to my adoptive family.

At first we lived in a flat in Ibrox, but soon we moved to a modest, semi-detached bungalow in King's Park. It could have been quite a nice house, had things been otherwise, but, as it was, the house was in a perpetual mess, which was always very distressing to me. The small lounge was to the left of the front door, the main bedroom to the right; the dining-room with French windows and steps into the back garden was on the right at the back, and between the dining-room and the kitchen was a single bedroom. There was a stair up to a small box-room and quite a large room, which was made into a bedroom for my sister. I learned many years later that she had been frightened up there by herself.

My mother owned the house, which was paid for by her father. This was not a happy situation for my father. I slept with my mother in the double bed in the front bedroom. My father slept in a single bed in the back bedroom.

No one seemed to know and I certainly could never find out how it was that my father and mother got together. Nowadays there would be an immediate divorce but, in those days, and because my mother was the kind of person she was, divorce was not an option. The overwhelming disgrace of it all was evidently something that could not be faced.

At the age of 6 with Bobby Bruin and in my arms, Gibson, who was a girl bear!

At the age of five I developed enteric fever - paratyphoid B, I believe it was, to be exact. Tests were carried out but the source was never discovered and no one else in the area developed it. At the time it was a complete mystery. I was taken by ambulance to Belvidere Hospital and, although I can remember it clearly, I do not recall how long I was there but it certainly seemed a very long time. No one could visit me but I remember Henry the postman -

kind soul that he was - came to the ward window to wave to me specially. We had a nanny - I'll explain about her later - and, as she was a trained nurse, she was allowed to visit - the one and only exception. She used to go to the nearby King's Park and pinch flowers! I got snowdrops from her and I remember vividly asking if I could have them beside me. I was told I was selfish! What a thing to say to a very ill, frightened five-year-old. A tiny little vase of snowdrops was not going to be noticed much in a large ward of very sick people. I remember being asked by a nice nurse what my favourite music was. She no doubt expected me to mention some childish song but I surprised everyone by replying 'Henry Hall'. There were no antibiotics in those days so recovery was very slow and all my soft toys had to be destroyed. However, recover I did. Jane and I both had all the usual childhood ailments.

At one time I had a black and white rabbit that I named 'Oswald St Johnicle.' Poor Oswald developed a tumour in his ear, so he did not last long. I do not know where the name came from but I was rather good at that sort of thing.

I used to invent games for Jane and me to play. Of course, I was always the boss and she was the underling. I remember deciding one day that Jane was to be my dog, Rover, so I tied a bit of string round her and she had to crawl about beside me. What awful cheek! Years later, I apologised to Jane for these episodes but she said she loved every minute of these games.

When Jane was about fourteen or so she developed meningitis and she was whisked away into Killearn Hospital to be under the eminent brain specialist, Eric Paterson. The war was on and there were very few buses available. My mother and I were stuffed into a single-decker, standing all the way usually. In those days,

Killearn was a long way from the south side of Glasgow. I remember being utterly shocked at seeing the other cases of meningitis in the wards and thinking that Jane was going to end up like them. However, penicillin had just come into use and the only way you could get it was by means of a drip into a vein in the leg and that was what saved Jane. But she told me years later that after she recovered from the meningitis she did not feel the same somehow.

It was a common occurrence that we would be suddenly snatched up by our mother and given a suppository. This was humiliating, degrading and probably quite unnecessary.

We were brought up to feel that we were quite worthless and that it was a terrible disgrace to be adopted. I used to wonder what exactly it had to do with me, but that's the way it was. Nothing was ever discussed or commented on. We had virtually no visitors and felt very isolated. During the war Jane and I collected for the Red Cross round the block. We were told not to go into anyone's house but, of course, we were invited in and often given a sweet. I used to love to see other people's houses because they were usually nicely furnished and tidy and ours was not. I used to be thrilled to see a lovely pink bedroom, for example.

Inevitably we played occasionally with neighbouring children but this was disapproved of and very much discouraged. One day a wee girl followed us into the kitchen and later my mother told me sternly 'Don't you ever dare to bring that girl in again'. I could not understand what harm I had done.

As a child, you are a prisoner. There is no escape from your predicament. I used to tremble at these lines from Psalm 148:

> *'And from that place,*
> *Where fix'd you be*
> *By his decree,*
> *You cannot pass.'*

All too true, unfortunately.

2 - My Father

'A man more sinned against than sinning'
(Shakespeare, *King Lear*)

My father was quite a good-looking man - tall, dark-haired with a moustache and a military bearing. His father had had an antiques business in Penrith, but I have no idea why he moved to Glasgow. After his wife died, he had married again and his second wife was always referred to as 'the Madre'. The family lived in a posh terrace in the West End of Glasgow. It was the sort of household where it would be 'roast on Sundays, cold on Mondays, hash on Tuesdays, rissoles on Wednesdays'. However, I really know very little about it. In any case we were not encouraged to get to know anything. Everything was surrounded with an aura of mystery.

My father was the elder of two brothers. He himself was very far from normal but his younger brother was married with two daughters. We rarely saw them. When the Madre died, our aunt asked my mother if there were any items of jewellery left, as 'she had real daughters'. There was in fact nothing, but my mother was furious about this remark.

My father had been in the Royal Flying Corps and had been shot down over France. He suffered from shellshock, as it was called then, and was left with the worst stutter I have ever encountered. It required a lot of patience to deal with this because I used to know what he was going to say long before he said it, but he just simply had to struggle to get his statement out himself every single time. It was one of the many tragedies in his life.

He was also an epileptic, though I never saw a fit. He took bromide for it and carried a bottle around with him. He was a very talented artist. He did etchings and he was Curator of Prints and Drawings in Kelvingrove Art Gallery and Museum in Glasgow. He had an entry in an ancient copy of *Who's Who in Art* which mentions his studies in Europe and his one-man shows. He was a great admirer of Rembrandt. When I was about seven I presented the bouquet to the lady invited to present the prizes to the winners of the art competition held each year in the Gallery. There was a terrible episode when my father was accused of drinking on the job and was likely to be sacked but he had only been drinking his bromide. Eventually the whole thing blew over, much to our relief.

My father did not come home for lunch, or for his evening meal - ever. I have no idea what he did but he was away all day and all evening. I think he went to the theatre or to the cinema night after night. I expect he did not want to come home. There was nothing to come home to.

During the evening my mother, Jane and I would be in the small front lounge. Then all of a sudden we would hear the garden gate and the feet on the gravel. My mother tensed up immediately. My father would come straight to the back door, let himself in and go into his bedroom at the back. He never came near us. Nevertheless, my mother displayed such an unwarranted fear of him which she transmitted to me. I never knew what Jane thought, because nothing was ever discussed. Thereafter my father went to bed, and the next day would be the same.

My father's bedroom was small. Once a single bed and a small wardrobe were in position, there was not much room for anything else. But there was a fret saw and bits of balsa wood lying about, as he was always trying to make models - usually unsuccessfully. He did not appear to have any friends but in any case, they would never have been brought home.

Very often Jane and I had to 'tidy Daddy's room'. This was a hopeless task, as it was in a perpetual state of untidiness and this was a pretty miserable occupation for a child. Now and then I used to hear skelping sounds coming from his room. One day I opened the door of his wardrobe and found that it was full of whips. Would they ever be used on Jane and me, I wondered? As a child it was well-nigh impossible for me to work out what all that was about. Later, of course - much, much later - I realised that he was a masochist and was interested in using the whips only on himself. Nothing was mentioned... no comment was made by anyone ever... nothing was ever explained.

Our nanny - whom we called Nurse - used to say many years later that Daddy was fond of us and would never have harmed us. I know he was latterly very proud of me and when I graduated he gave me a lovely etching of the University of Glasgow by Wilfred Appleby, which I still have on a wall today.

During World War II my father joined the RAF. My mother was delighted at the prospect of getting rid of him for a bit. Imagine her dismay and horror when she saw him walking down the hill towards our house - he had been posted to Renfrew - only a few miles away! Later he was in 'maps' in Sierra Leone so she did in fact get rid of him for a while. When I reached years of maturity I used to think that service life was what he was really suited to. I am sure he would have been happier as a permanent airman, had that been possible.

After returning to the Art Gallery, after the war, eventually my father had to retire. He was succeeded by Alasdair Auld, who later became the Director of Kelvingrove. I remember when he came to the house one day - a man of considerable charm.

So now my father sat all the time alone in the dining-room, watching the television. My mother was always in the lounge, listening to the radio which blared constantly. I never heard a word of complaint from him and, as I grew older, I tried very hard to be as kind to him as I could be.

After I graduated from University, he suffered a stroke, and I visited him in the nursing-home. He was always pleased to see me and would say things like 'Katharine, you're very busy, so don't you worry about coming here' which was an enormous contrast to the constant complaints I would get from my mother. This made me remember him with affection.

The way my mother treated him was absolutely shocking. She treated him with contempt. He never stood up to her... he did not seem to have any fight in him. Looking back on it all, I find it all so very sad. He was a poor, poor soul.

3 - My Mother

An impossible person, not worthy of the name.

I can think of no one less deserving of the name. She had no idea of the meaning of the word love. Her father was a well-to-do lawyer in Glasgow. He had been a widower for some time so we never knew his wife. My mother was their only child.

Grandpa lived in quite a large semi-detached house in Dumbreck. I remember it well. He had two maids - Big Bella and Wee Bella - and the rumour (if indeed it was a rumour) was that Big Bella was a lot more than just a maid. When he was dying, it was Big Bella he wanted, certainly not my mother.

Remembering Big Bella reminds me of the day she and her friend, Annie, took Jane and me to the Empire Exhibition in 1938 in Bellahouston Park, quite near Grandpa's house. They had specially asked if they could take us and we were told that we had to do whatever they wanted and visit whatever pavilions they wished to see. But, of course, it was not like that at all and we were at the Fun Fair all the time. I remember particularly all four of us squashed into a Waltzer. We had a lovely time and so did they. It was amazing that we were allowed to do this at all.

When we were at a small Kindergarten in Shawlands we used to be taken to Dumbreck in the bus most Thursdays for lunch. Grandpa was never there as he was at business. We always had stewed gigot chops with carrot, turnip and onion. I can taste it yet! I have no idea, however, why we had these visits to Dumbreck.

My mother's attitude to her father was most odd. They did not even seem to be fond of each other. Possibly the reason their relationship was so poor, was that he was known to be a womaniser, and his wife died in agony of gonorrhoea.

In fact, Grandpa knew his daughter well and, when he died, his money was left in trust to Jane and me until we came of age, and, until then, my mother had the interest for life. Clearly there was no way she was going to be entrusted with his money, and the whole arrangement caused her great displeasure. Her attitude to us, as a result, was sour and complaining, as if we had somehow been responsible for it all. However, had it not been for Grandpa, things would have been so much more difficult, because there was never any money for us. My mother was always talking poor-mouth and this rubbed off on me and made me feel more insecure than ever.

I was regarded by her as her property. Whether she even liked me or not was beside the point. She did not like Jane, who was largely ignored, and Jane loathed her. My mother absolutely hated men. My father was treated merely as a lodger in the house. She disliked him intensely and was irrationally afraid of him, though there was never any evidence of a reason for such a situation. The whole business of sex repulsed her.

As I mentioned earlier, I slept with my mother in the double bed in the master bedroom. This was a ghastly arrangement for me, as I never, ever got away from her. The unfortunate spin-off from this was that Jane thought I was in cahoots with my mother but nothing could have been further from the truth. I should have been sleeping upstairs with Jane, but there was no way my mother was going to give us the opportunity to get pally and gang up against her. She took good care to keep us separate.

As I grew older, I became more and more like her slave. The awful disgrace of being illegitimate and the fact that I should be intensely grateful to her for adopting me was always much to the fore. This made me feel that I must 'pay her back' in some way, such as by working hard to be a credit to her. Whenever there was any sign of someone showing an interest in us or wanting to be friendly, it was quickly nipped in the bud. No encouragement was ever given to anyone to become friendly.

Latterly, any spare time that I had was expected to be devoted to her. She made demands on me in a totally unreasonable way. For example, if I said I was going out on a certain evening, she would immediately say that she wanted me to wash and set her hair that very night. This, of course, had the desired effect of making me feel guilty, although the hair-do could easily have waited for another night.

However, I very soon learned that I could never please her. She had a tiresome habit of speaking in clichés all the time. If she saw me carrying a lot of items she would immediately say 'That's a lazy man's burden', but if, on the other hand, I was only lightly loaded she would be telling me that I should be 'making my head save my feet'. I could not win.

Jane and I were told that we must never ever speak to anyone about the situation at home. It was so strange that it was most unlikely that we would and, in any case, what friends were we ever allowed to have to talk to? No one was supposed to know what went on but years later I realised that folk knew much more than we thought they did. The onlooker sees most of the game. For example, at secondary school no one in my class was supposed to know I was adopted but I discovered eventually that my class-mates had known all along. Did it really matter so much?

My birthday was never known for certain and had to be a guess but my mother even made my birthday the same as hers. I used to think that was a very odd thing indeed - almost unbelievable. She would not allow me to see my birth certificate but the day came, when I was in my twenties, when I had to produce it for my employers. It was then that I discovered that the date on the document was in fact four days later in the month. Can you imagine what a fool I felt with my employers? There I was in a responsible job and I did not even know the date of my own birthday.

My mother also falsified Jane's birthday as well. She was actually ten months younger than I, her birthday month being September. But my mother felt that the two births were unnaturally close, so Jane's birthday month was changed to December. So, when we were in our twenties we had to be doing some adjustments. This whole business was so bizarre and caused us a lot of totally unnecessary distress.

There was no way that my mother could ever have run a house. She did not have a clue. She spent most of the time doing nothing but listening to the radio which blared perpetually. She could not cook. The only thing I remember her making was jelly which was put outside on the window-sill to set, where it gathered all sorts of specks from the atmosphere. No fridge, of course, in those days and no central heating. When you left the coal fire in the lounge you were perished to death in the rest of the house in winter.

Now, this is where I want to explain about our nanny, whom we called Nurse. She was a permanent fixture, and slept in the box-room. It was doubtful if my mother could have functioned without her. It said an awful lot for her that she stayed with us for so long. My mother needed a scapegoat too so it was handy to blame Nurse when anything went wrong.

Nurse was in fact a trained nurse and she had a sister, who was a district nurse, and they lived in a flat in Ibrox, with the biggest aspidistra in the world in the lounge. Nurse was a most loyal servant and was very fond of us. She was also a very good cook, which was such a blessing in our barren household. Once a week Nurse went home to Ibrox for a few hours to see her sister. Occasionally, as a special treat, I was allowed to go home with Nurse. She always went out to shop in Paisley Road West and that was when I got to choose a cake for my tea. What a thrill! The strange thing is that I have no recollection of Jane ever being with us.

My mother had only one friend - a single lady, very comfortably off, who lived in a big house in Dumbreck. We called her 'Auntie Mabel'. She was a kindly person and was very fond of us. One year she asked me what I would like for Christmas - I suppose I must have been about seven at the time - and I replied immediately, 'Beads and perfume!' Needless to say, this resulted in a row from my mother, who said I had no right to ask for such things. I could not understand what the fuss was about as I had given a straight answer to a straight question, which I am sure was very helpful to Auntie Mabel. We each got a beautiful little necklace with pale green beads and a bottle of eau de Cologne from Woolworth's!

Auntie Mabel, a most loyal friend, was absolutely the only person who ever visited us, even if only occasionally. She was smart enough to see a bit of what was going on and, many years later, she said to me 'I often wanted to take you home with me'. I used to accompany Auntie Mabel to the bus-stop when she went home. One day I said to her that I thought it was awful that she always got a pie and beans for her tea. 'Oh,' she said, 'don't worry about that. I'd rather have that than your mother's cooking'.

I never said a nasty word to my mother... I never asked her anything, accused her of anything, or complained about anything. I just suffered in silence and that was my big problem. There was no one to talk to.

4 - My Sister

A sad victim of circumstances

From the various comments I have made about Jane, you will already have some idea of what she was like. To say that I loved her would, sadly, not be true. However, I cared a great deal about her and always felt very concerned about her, but we were never allowed to be close.

Jane was always very difficult. You never knew what she was thinking or feeling. When people are open about their opinions and so on, things always seem so much easier. You know where you are with them, but I never knew where I was with Jane. For one thing, I do not think she had a clue about me and I suppose the situation at home was enough to make one feel suspicious about everything. Never at any time did I blame her for this. She had her personality problems as I had mine.

We both went to piano lessons for several years to a lady who lived within walking distance. She enjoyed a splendid reputation as an excellent teacher, but that did not prevent us from being afraid of her. (I expect she would have been most surprised to hear that!) She had so many pupils that an examiner from the Associated Board came to her house. We always had lessons in the front downstairs room but, when it got near exam time, we had a few weeks of lessons on the posh piano upstairs to enable us to get used to it before our exam. Jane was never willing to play in public but she did get her qualification from Trinity College, London (ATCL) and it was hoped that she would take over the piano school when our teacher retired. I remember Jane had a very few pupils in our house but she was quite hopeless as a teacher and there was no system in place for collecting the fees, which just got forgotten about. In any case, her heart was simply not in it.

We both took refuge in religion but in totally different ways. We first went to King's Park Parish Church of Scotland, but Jane did not last long there. She joined the local Episcopalian Church but that did not last long either and she became a Roman Catholic. As far as our mother was concerned, this was a disaster of the first order as, like many people in Glasgow at that time, she was bitterly anti-Roman Catholics. That was not something I could easily understand, because one's religion was usually an accident of birth and, in Jane's case, I felt that someone in her early twenties was entitled to make up her own mind. The only thing about it all that saddened me greatly was that Jane refused thereafter to recognise any Church of Scotland minister. She had now made the decision to go, as it were, where she knew no one from the family would follow her.

After the abortive attempt to be a piano teacher, Jane did what she really wanted to do. She trained as a nurse in the Victoria Infirmary, not so very far away in Battlefield. Prior to this, she had become a VAD and was so good at it that 'Pop Burton', a famous surgeon in the Royal Infirmary at the time, allowed Jane to attend his operations. It was absolutely unheard of for such a thing to happen. Jane told me that her experience of being in Killearn Hospital with meningitis had made her resolve to be a nurse. The effect on me, however, was the exact opposite!

Having qualified as a nurse, Jane worked at the Victoria Infirmary for a while. She also nursed in Canniesburn where a top consultant said she was the best nurse in the place. However, the very sad thing was that two flaws went against her. First she never seemed to like any of her colleagues - she seldom liked anybody in fact - and second, she was unable to accept responsibility and never became a Sister when she could easily have done so.

She had a tendency to pal up with folk who were decidedly odd. I used to think that she had to accept friendship where she found it. She met a married couple who were planning to walk through Europe to Bombay. He was Indian and she was German or Austrian, I think. Jane decided to join them in this extraordinary trek. Had she been so inclined, this would have been a marvellous opportunity to write a weekly article for a newspaper or magazine, describing the various stages of the journey, but there was no question of that. I know nothing about that journey. She was incommunicado. There was no way I could write to her and she was such a poor correspondent that she did not write to me. Perhaps she thought - quite mistakenly - that I was not interested. Eventually we heard that she was working in a hospital run by nuns in Bombay. Although I now had an address for her and did write fairly regularly I did not get a reply. After eight months I wrote to say that if I did not hear from her by return I was going to write to the Mother Superior. That produced a reply!

Jane was in Bombay for several years but eventually the situation in India changed and she decided it was time to come home. I knew that she had a great desire to become a nun and so I was pleased for her when she was accepted as a novice in a Benedictine Abbey in North Wales. Luckily she liked the Mistress of Novices, who later became the Abbess, and that was a tremendous plus for Jane. It could easily have been otherwise.

I visited her annually. At first I could speak with her only across a wooden counter with a wooden grid hanging above it. The grid was never lowered, as it would have been in the past, as things were not as strict as they had once been. Eventually I was at her Solemn Profession, when her final vows were taken and she was fully accepted into the community. After that, she was kept in seclusion for some time. The Benedictine Order is a closed order and silence is observed. There was, for example, no speaking at meals and only essential speaking at other times. When the fabric of the building in North Wales began to give concern, a move to England was planned. When the new Abbess took over, the atmosphere was more relaxed. I always got a great welcome from the nuns when I visited the convent and enjoyed conversation with many of them in turn in the parlour. They were and are a group of talented women. I still keep up with them - particularly with the Abbess through correspondence. It was a great privilege to be allowed to visit a closed order in that way.

One day Jane had a heart attack and then a stroke which left her unable to swallow. For two years she lay in bed with liquid food being pumped into her by means of a stomach peg. The care she got from the Abbess and the nuns was absolutely wonderful and I will never cease to be grateful for it. When she slipped away at last, I could not help feeling relieved that she was out of her misery.

I hope Jane found some sort of happiness as a nun, though it was always hard to tell what she was feeling. She would not have been the easiest of persons to have around so it was all credit to her fellow nuns for coping with her. It was very fortunate that she was accepted into the community. Had this not been the case, I could not have imagined her in a small flat looking after herself, as she was so undomesticated. Her interest in cooking was nil and in India she had become a vegetarian.

When I reflect on Jane's life - my mother's dislike of her - indeed her antagonism to her and her total lack of sympathy or understanding - the whole thing is a great sadness to me.

5 - Education, Education, Education

*'It's what remains, if one has forgotten everything
one learned in school.'* (Albert Einstein)

The first school we went to was Woodholm School, which was a large house in Langside. I do not remember my first day there but I have clear memories of trying to cultivate a tiny patch of the garden; the ash playground that was so cruel on your knees, if you fell; the assembly room, which seemed like a baronial hall but was, no doubt, only a large room; and the French lessons - even at that age - from a real, live Frenchman, Monsieur D.

Madame Souris a une maison. La maison de Madame Souris est petite.

My most vivid memories, however, are of the headmistress, Miss McVey, who inspired in me something akin to devotion. She held a party once at school, appearing in a gorgeous, tangerine taffeta frock with bows down the front. There was a romantic ending to all this, for Miss McVey got engaged to a Frenchman (not Monsieur D!) and went to live in Paris. I remember her engagement ring was a pearl with diamonds. Of course we gave her a gift and while we were all waiting in a queue to be kissed good-bye, I distinguished myself by letting out one mighty bawl and starting the whole school crying!

The only pupil I remember was a nice wee girl called Moira Duff. Her father drove her to school in his Alvis, which had a brass hare on the front as a mascot. I adored this hare and kind Mr Duff managed to give me one, which is still one of my most treasured possessions. I hope I was polite and showed my appreciation of such a kindly gesture.

After Woodholm School we went to another small private school in Strathbungo called Moray House. It was a house in a terrace. The headmistress was a Miss Walker, who also owned Radleigh School in Giffnock. Occasionally we had to go there, if there was a problem at Moray House, such as frozen pipes. I do not recall ever being taught by Miss Walker. Our teacher was Miss Anderson and we had more or less one-to-one tuition as it was a very small school. I liked Miss Anderson. She had two rather stern tweed suits which she wore regularly to school. Both were of similar pale yellow and brown colours, one with a small hound's tooth check and the other with a more open check. Sometimes at the end of school we would see her leaving and she always had a hat on and a fox fur over one shoulder. How I loved that fur!

When we got too old for Moray House, our education seemed to be a bit of a problem. The war was starting and we went to the local secondary school. For a while we had lessons in different houses in the district and sat round a big table, presumably in the dining-room. My teacher was a drab-looking, middle-aged woman called Mrs Macaulay. When she appeared when we were all outside waiting to go into the house, someone would shout out, 'Here comes collie-dog!' Later I was in the school building for a while in an enormous class.

However, this was when Grandpa stepped in and said we must go to the Park School for Girls in Lynedoch Street, near Charing Cross in Glasgow. My mother had been there. However worthless she thought we were, Grandpa seemed to think that we deserved a good education and he paid for it, of course. We went to school by bus, getting off in Woodlands Road at the foot of Lynedoch Lane, which we walked up. There were about twenty girls in each class and the form mistress might change from year to year. The teachers were all spinsters - the men were away at the war. The dedication these women showed was exemplary but it was hard work all the time. Looking back, I do not think that anybody knew the meaning of the word 'fun' but perhaps that was because of the wartime conditions. Most of us were frightened of the staff. They were an intimidating lot, though they themselves were completely unaware of this, as we discovered many years later. The headmistress taught mathematics and woe betide you if you got 'see me' at the end of your homework. The senior French mistress was furious if we made a mistake with irregular verbs dished out as homework. I used to think it was a bit unreasonable, but it certainly kept us on our toes.

I was good at French and was often complimented on my accent. When inspectors came, we had to be ready to recite something in French. While the others got parts of French poems to learn, I was given a prose passage by Victor Hugo - 'Le Retrait de Moscou'. The only bit of it I remember is 'il neigeait' which had to be said with some weight, as if you were feeling the weight of the snow.

Over the years I got several prizes for French. Just as we were about to leave school, some very limited foreign travel began to be allowed and a trip to Paris was arranged for those and such as those, but I was not selected. I never knew why, but it was rather hurtful at the time.

I liked Latin a lot and used to get 100% in the exams, which always made my class-mates gasp. One day I happened to meet the Latin mistress in the lane and I said to her that I would like to learn

Greek. She immediately arranged to teach me - one-to-one of course - in the lunch hour and after two years I passed in Higher Greek and got prizes for it too. I do not think she had ever had the opportunity to teach Greek before. It was indeed good of her to give up her lunch hours in that way. I hope I showed some enthusiastic appreciation. In those days, of course, it was not possible for me to show appreciation to anyone in any tangible way because I had no money and I never asked for any.

When we were in our late teens, Jane and I went every Saturday night to the orchestral concerts in St Andrew's Hall. It was the Scottish Orchestra in those days before it became the Scottish National Orchestra. Jane had been having violin lessons and she had a crush on Jean Rennie, the leader. We particularly liked the conductor, Walter Susskind, who was also a fine pianist. He often played a Mozart piano concerto, conducting the orchestra from the piano. We knew by name and had heard most of the well-known musicians of the day and I have many autographs. There were comparatively few of them - probably because of restricted travel. Today, however, they are so numerous and come from all over the world. The pleasure Jane and I got from these concerts was enormous and they contributed greatly to our education and instilled a love of music in me which has lasted all my life.

My memories of World War II are very limited. We shared a small rectangular air-raid shelter built on to the French windows in our dining-room and also on to the French windows of our neighbours' dining-room. Looking back at the situation, I feel that it was not likely to be very beneficial, but, thankfully, we were never required to put it to the test. Our neighbours were Mr and Mrs Craig and her brother Mr Burns. The great excitement for us was seeing Mrs Craig, who was rather a large lady, in her nightie, when we were up during the night. Mr Burns played the cello and latterly he would come in and play trios with Jane on the violin and me on the piano. It must have sounded awful. I was much keener on that sort of thing than Jane was, as you can probably guess.

Although I was very academic, I absolutely loathed physical education in any form whatsoever. I used to feel sore after it too. Stripping was also a bit of a nightmare for me, as I suffered from excessive hair on my arms, legs and lip. This might have been the result of an over-active suprarenal gland or of a tumour of its cortex. The over-production of androgen hormones can produce excess growth of hair, but at that stage nothing was done about it. Of course, I was powerless to take any action to alleviate my intense misery, but later, when I was in my twenties I went to an eminent endocrinologist and had various tests in Stobhill Hospital. They were all negative, so the consultant said the condition was hereditary, and were my father and mother hairy? No one could know that, so I was told that my biological father and mother must both have been hairy. I spent many years with hair-erasing pads and, when I was able to pay for it, I attended the Tao Clinic in Glasgow to have my lip treated. At first the visits were very frequent but eventually they became less necessary and finally ceased. There is no doubt that electrolysis was the answer and I was so glad that I was able to have that treatment on the part that was always on view.

Another thing I did not enjoy at school was being a Girl Guide. I was in the school company and the captain was the Latin mistress. She always gave me the nod to start off singing taps at the end of the meeting. She was a most distinguished guider, a Commissioner with the Medal of Merit, which on certain occasions hung over the precipice of her ample bosom. The fact that I liked her and respected her so much kept me going. We had a weekend camp once at the Mains Estate, Milngavie. That was my idea of hell - rain pouring down, horrible drippy tents, creepy crawlies and ghastly food. Mrs Douglas of Mains was a very senior guider and she lived in the big house on the estate. Our captain asked me to take a message to her and I still have a vivid memory of the nice welcome I got. Mrs Douglas took me into her house and showed me her octagonal bedroom, which I thought was just wonderful.

In my early teens I decided I wanted to do something towards the war effort. I do not remember how this came about but an arrangement was made for me to wash dishes for two hours on a Saturday morning in a former hotel in the Cowcaddens, which had been converted into a NAAFI canteen. The lady in charge, Mrs Cuthill, was exceptionally nice. Things were fine as long as the water was hot, but sometimes this did not last and it was an unpleasant struggle dealing with greasy dishes with only tepid water. I was always being asked if I would like to wait at the tables instead but I never felt up to that somehow and was quite glad to be in the background. I do not remember how long this went on for, but I am sure I was considered a bit of an oddity. When the war was over, I got a war service badge from the Guides. This was a little embroidered gold crown on a navy blue ribbon which had to be stitched on to the left side of my uniform at the front. I never came across anyone else with one.

When I was at Park School I had one particular friend in the class but more of her anon. I was at her house for tea once or twice. But, although I felt friendly enough towards the other girls I was never invited to their homes and they were not particularly friendly to me. The only telephone calls I got were from class-mates wondering if I had managed to do the maths or work out the Latin translation we'd been given as homework. It was quite obvious to me that these telephone calls were not evidence of popularity. They were just an easy way of solving their problems.

I sat my Highers, got them all, and now it was time to leave for Glasgow University and the big wide world. But first, a little musical interlude.

6 - An Ill Wind That Nobody Blows Good
Purely a matter of opinion

And that was indeed Danny Kaye's opinion of the oboe which I took up when I was seventeen. The only instrument available was a very old one that was not much good, but I could not get a teacher either. (Changed days today with everything laid on a plate!) An advert produced a reply from the bandmaster in Maryhill Barracks and I went there for some time. It was always exciting and fun passing the sentry.

The band master was a very nice man but he was a bassoon-player, which was not ideal, even although I knew that at Kneller Hall bandmasters were trained to teach all brass and woodwind instruments. I also learned a bit of harmony from him, now long forgotten, I am afraid. The situation was not ideal and eventually I was put in touch with a very nice elderly oboist in Cardonald. He was a most kindly teacher but he died suddenly and his oboe was bought for me from a relative of the deceased. Somewhat unusually, it was a Heckel oboe; Heckel made bassoons. Most of the oboes in use then were French and the Heckel mechanism was slightly different. That did not bother me at all. It was a very fine instrument.

I started to go to the Saturday morning orchestral class in the old Athenaeum, which became the Royal Scottish Academy of Music and Drama (RSAMD). The orchestra was trained by Horace Fellowes, who was a very well-known violinist. I believe he had known Grandpa, so that was a help to me in some ways. He arranged for me to get lessons from an oboist in the BBC and that was a great improvement.

When I started at Glasgow University I went right away to join the University Orchestra. There were other oboists there and I remember one in particular. He became a doctor and about sixty years later, as I remembered his name, I discovered that I was sitting beside his sister-in-law at a lunch in the Western Club in Glasgow, although I never met him again. However, I was immediately head-hunted by an amateur musician, who begged me to join the Glasgow Orchestral Society. I protested and pointed out that I was completely inexperienced but he said they were desperate for an oboist and refused to take no for an answer.

And so I did not go back to the Glasgow University Orchestra but became the Glasgow Orchestral Society's first oboe for the next twenty or so years while keeping up my lessons. There were many nice people in the orchestra, which was conducted by J Peebles Conn, a well-known violinist. He was a most kindly, gentlemanly person and a helpful and sympathetic conductor. We rehearsed in the Mid Hall of St Andrew's Halls, an ideal venue. We had two concerts a year in the main hall with a professional soloist. Over the years I played a great deal of the standard repertoire. I was always in demand and many of us used to help out the Greenock Amateur Orchestra at their concert. Traditionally, Gilbert and Sullivan operas were performed by Lanarkshire schools in those days and I often played for them. After a week in the orchestral pit, I knew the lyrics off by heart! It was all very valuable experience and I was also attending the RSAMD orchestral practices on Saturdays.

I was never much interested in pin-ups but my great hero was Léon Goossens, the brilliant oboist. He seldom came to Scotland but in 1950 he was the soloist one weekend with the Scottish National Orchestra. The Friday concert was in Edinburgh's Usher Hall and the Saturday one in Glasgow's St Andrew's Hall. I decided to go to both concerts to get a double dose of Léon Goossens and, at the interval in Glasgow, I was fortunate in getting an opportunity to see him and I got him to sign a photograph of himself that I had cut out of a magazine. I still have it framed on my piano. He was an absolute marvel. I was also able on one occasion to speak to Evelyn Rothwell, John Barbirolli's wife, who had made a name for herself as a solo oboist. They were such an odd-looking couple as John Barbirolli was quite small and Evelyn Rothwell was exceptionally tall. Another brilliant oboe soloist was Heinz Holliger.

In December 1954, *The Scotsman's* music critic said of me that 'the first oboe was worthy of note'. The symphony on that occasion had been Schubert's Great C Major. In May 1955 Horace Fellowes organised a concert to mark his eightieth birthday, the orchestra consisting of his pupils and friends. At that concert I played Handel's G minor Oboe Concerto - 'a promising exponent of this very tricky instrument,' said the review.

In November 1958, I was described in a headline in *The Glasgow Herald* as a 'Promising Young Oboist' - in a report of the Glasgow String Orchestra's concert in St Andrew's Hall, at which I played Vivaldi's D minor Oboe Concerto and the Corelli Concerto, which could be more accurately described as a suite of dance movements. My playing was described as 'always admirably neat and thoughtfully phrased'. A school for conductors and orchestral players was held at Jordanhill College about this time and I attended that, as Horace Fellowes was in charge.

I still have the relevant cuttings in my scrap book.

We used to have Chamber Music Evenings now and then, which gave the members of the Glasgow Orchestral Society an opportunity to perform something different. On these occasions I used to play oboe concerti with a string quartet - usually Vivaldi, as his compositions lent themselves to this sort of combination instead of a full string orchestra.

Two friends, who played clarinet and bassoon, and I formed a trio. (We never gave ourselves a name. That was very unlike me!) There is a very good repertoire for this combination and we were often invited to play at various events. I remember how difficult it was to find an evening when we were all free for practice because, of course, we all had jobs. It was even worse when we played with a horn and a flute as a wind quintet.

On 23rd October 1962 St Andrew's Hall burned down. The cause of this terrible tragedy was reputed to have been a cigarette at a boxing match. At the time, I was President of the Glasgow Orchestral Society and I and my committee had to take immediate action to find another venue for rehearsals. We had always used St Andrew's Mid Hall, so we lost property in the fire, in particular a large quantity of music. We were fortunate in getting accommodated in the Bible Training Institute, which was in Bothwell Street at the time.

Nadia Boulanger, the famous French musician and teacher, advised her pupils 'not to take up music unless you would rather die than not do so'. Sir Thomas Beecham, the conductor, famed for his outspokenness and wit, said that 'the function of music is to release us from the tyranny of conscious thought'. The quotations about music are legion and there is no doubt that it soothed my savage breast.

Some years later I found myself becoming aware of a hostile atmosphere in the orchestra. It was very strange and I could not understand it. I became more and more nervous at rehearsals. Then one day, out of the blue, I got a telephone call from a member of the orchestra to say that they wanted rid of me. A petition was drawn up against this, by some of the members, but to no avail. I decided to resign immediately, as I did not see what else I could do. It was an awful heartbreak. This kind of thing does happen. I knew of at least two musicians, both professionals, who experienced something similar.

I did not play my oboe again but I kept it for years afterwards. I know it sounds silly but somehow I could not bear to part with it. Eventually common sense prevailed and I gave my instrument to the woodwind section of the Royal Conservatoire of Scotland in Glasgow.

7 - University and My First Two Jobs

My alma mater and becoming an editor

In 1948 I left school and went to Glasgow University to do an Arts Degree. It should have been a great, fulfilling experience for me but it wasn't. I was beginning to be nervously and emotionally ill. Instead of enjoying every minute of my studies it was taking me all my time to keep going. I had to study with the radio blaring, as my mother refused to do without it. We had no central heating so the only warmth was from the coal fire in the small lounge. The other rooms were all very cold. Instead of branching out and joining University clubs, I could not cope with anything extra and I spent most of my time in Queen Margaret Union.

I used to go to the Chapel each morning for the ten-minute service. The Principal, Sir Hector Hetherington, was always there. I remember vividly the Rev Archibald Craig, the first University chaplain, who later - as Moderator of the General Assembly of the Church of Scotland - was the first to be granted a papal visit. The story goes that when he was saying farewell to Pope John XXIII he said, 'So long, John,' and the Pope replied, 'Arrivederci, Erchie'.

Instead of making lots of new friends I kept myself to myself. It was almost impossible for me to know what to do to improve things. I am still in touch with two people from those far-off days but scarcely in a big way.

I graduated in 1952. How I ever got through anything is a mystery to me. As I said before, my father was proud of me and gave me an etching of the University by Wilfred Appleby but he was not allowed to come to the graduation ceremony. Only two tickets were permitted per person and my mother and Jane attended. I was not allowed to have a photograph in colour. My mother said we could not afford it.

It was quite obvious to me that the first essential was to get a job and earn some money. I consulted the Student Advisory Service and it so happened that Glasgow University Press - Robert MacLehose & Co, the printers - wanted someone to proofread Latin and Greek and I got the job right away. This meant travelling quite a long way from the south side of Glasgow to Anniesland Cross. I think my salary was £360 per annum and even in those days that was very poor.

Glasgow University Press printed a great many Latin and Greek texts and also all the examination papers which had to be proofread. It was a huge printing works with Monotype and Linotype machines with the metal bubbling in them. The men who looked after them were very proud of 'they machines' and there were comings and goings between them and the editorial staff.

The person in charge of us was a tiny wee man, called Willie Bryson, who was a dynamo. He used to say that he joined MacLehose as a wee boy and left as a wee man. I got on fine with him but I realised that he was not likely to stick up for me, if anything went wrong. Besides checking all the Latin and Greek I read other works as well. There were many interesting things printed there. I particularly enjoyed *The Proceedings of the Hudson Bay Company*. As there were so many complaints from the publishers about mistakes in *Gray's Anatomy* I was given these proofs to check as well. Of course, there were the Printers'

Readers - several men in a compartment in the factory with a Head Reader - and I do not think that this arrangement made me too popular with them at first, but later I got on fine with them too.

There was another graduate on the editorial staff and that was Lilias Scott, the daughter of Francis George Scott, the composer. I became quite friendly with her and I was invited to tea at the Scotts' house in Jordanhill. Lilias's father was a lecturer in music at Jordanhill College of Education and was famous for his songs. There was a son, Alexander, who was a teacher, and Mrs Scott was very pleasant but the whole visit was very bland. However, I cannot imagine that I myself was exactly sparkling. Lilias eventually went out to South Africa to marry the Scottish composer, Erik Chisholm, who was Professor of Music in Cape Town University. I lost touch with her then.

There were very few of us on the editorial staff, perhaps no more than three. If we found anything doubtful as a result of our checking, we were not allowed to send letters to the authors ourselves. I used to think that was ridiculous but that is how it was. Any query had to be raised by a Director. I recall vividly the time when I came across a Greek word that I was sure was incorrect. It would have been easy enough to deal with the matter myself, but not so easy to explain to someone who did not know Greek. However, this had to be done through the cocky son of one of the Directors. When the reply came back and I was proved right, he threw the letter at my desk saying, 'There you are. The author's amazed at your erudition'. To the Directors you were scarcely a human being and, if you were walking behind one of them and there were swing doors, you had to watch out.

Mistakes were not allowed, so I was brought up in a hard school but it was all excellent training for my next job. After two and a half years there, I was beginning to feel that the job was not stretching me, so I went back to the Student Advisory Service to see if I could get another job in which my experience would be useful. That very morning a letter had come in from Blackie & Son, the Publishers, requesting someone to edit their Latin publications. I got that job right away.

Blackie's were in Stanhope Street in the Townhead district of Glasgow, near Glasgow Cathedral. We often saw women pushing their prams with their washing on their way to the 'steamie'.

I had a huge square desk in the family library and the Science Editor worked at another desk nearby. Everything was very formal and first names were never used. In separate offices were two other young female editors, who dealt with other subjects and three art editors in another large room, as well as our boss, the Educational Manager, who had his own office. The chairman was Walter Graham Blackie, whose father had commissioned from Charles Rennie Mackintosh the Hill House in Helensburgh, where Walter and his sister were brought up. He was very keen on atlases and he would often come into the library to consult one. He suffered from a stomach complaint, for which he had a white powder, but that did not keep him from eating the sugar lumps at meetings!

Mr Walter Graham Blackie (left) with his charming wife, Nancy, talking to Mr Ian Collins of Collins the Publishers, at the time of Blackie's Sesquicentennial Celebrations, 1959.

We produced only educational books. Children's books were all produced in the London office. The other Director, who dealt with scientific publications, and who was the Science Editor's boss, was Harry Bisacre. There were two middle-aged ladies who were the Directors' secretaries. One of the first things I had to edit and see through the press was a four-book Latin grammar but over the years I dealt with many other books as well. We had to liaise with the art editors when deciding on illustrations. I was very poorly paid but I was quite happy in the job for most of the time.

However, I was far from well and was getting worse. Sometimes I felt panic-stricken and, if I met someone I knew on the bus, for example, I could not converse with them. I had to excuse myself - somewhat lamely. There were only two occasions when I could not even get on a bus and was absent from work, but somehow I managed to keep going. I could hardly eat and I used to live on milk with Milo (something like Ovaltine) sprinkled on it. My colleagues seemed unaware of my troubles.

Although we had always been severely discouraged from discussing anything to do with the situation at home, it got to the stage where I went to see our minister. The manse was nearby so it was quite easy to consult him there without causing protests at home. He was absolutely wonderful, kindly and supportive. One evening service I was so panic-stricken I had to leave. The following Sunday I sat at the end of a pew at the very back and, Sunday by Sunday, I worked my way forward until I was able to stay put for the length of the service in my usual pew. I did it, but it took some doing. Of course the minister knew what was going on.

Eventually he said to me that I should see a psychiatrist and as he knew the Medical Director of Leverndale Hospital he put me in touch with him. I went regularly to see him. Dr James Milne was a delightful man and I got on well with him but progress was so slow. A quick recovery could not be expected. Dr Milne asked me to write to him so I did that for quite a long time and found it very helpful. After so many years the substance of these visits is rather hazy, but I do remember clearly two comments that he made. The first was that I would be unlikely to make a satisfactory marriage and the second was that I had the sort of temperament that gets things done. While I found myself agreeing with the latter, I was not so sure about the former, which was a sad, discouraging assessment. After some time Dr Milne told me that it was essential for me to leave home as it was the cause of all my troubles. I left his office reeling from the blow, wondering how on earth I was going to cope.

8 - My New Life in Digs

Living in a room and kitchen

What next? Well, there was nothing so terribly special about leaving home. We know it happens all the time but perhaps in rather different and happier circumstances than those in which I found myself.

I started to look at the appropriate advertisements in the daily press and I soon came across one which said:

'Bed-sittingroom with own kitchen'

which I followed up right away. This turned out to be in a terraced house in Clarkston Road in Muirend, not so very far away. It was owned by a very nice lady called Mrs Fraser, whom I remember with great affection. She had been widowed and the only way she could afford to live there was by having lodgers. The room she was advertising was the front bedroom upstairs and the kitchen was halfway upstairs on the landing, next to the bathroom. The front lounge downstairs and the back bedroom upstairs were always let to a married couple awaiting their first house. They shared the large kitchen at the back downstairs with Mrs Fraser, who had the back room downstairs as a bed-sittingroom. It all seemed to work quite well.

What on earth Mrs Fraser thought of me that day I went to see her I cannot imagine. I must have looked awful - gaunt and thin as a rake. However, she accepted me and a date was fixed for my arrival. I have no idea now what I paid her weekly but it must have been well within my means. There was an arrangement about contributing to the cost of the gas and electricity and I was allowed a bath on a Friday night. If for any reason I was unable to take it, then that was just too bad. There was a telephone in the hall downstairs but I hardly ever used it and I discouraged incoming calls for me, unless they were absolutely essential.

I said very little to my mother. I never at any time discussed my feelings or my problems, nor did I tell her that she was responsible for all the misery Jane and I had experienced. I simply said that many girls of my age - I was twenty-four - liked to be independent, so I had got myself a wee place in Muirend and was moving there shortly. 'But don't worry,' I added. 'I'll be back to see you very soon'. I discovered later that my mother had immediately telephoned everybody I knew to tell them that I had gone mad and left home and not to have anything to do with me.

At that time I had very few possessions so I suppose my move was comparatively easy. I had my clothes; my books; my LPs and record-player; my oboe, music and music-stand; and my typewriter. I had to ask Mrs Fraser to lend me a cup, saucer and plate and some cutlery until I could afford to buy some of these essentials.

The room itself was fine with a single bed, a wardrobe, a dressing table in the oriel window, and a folding table which could seat four people. There was no central heating so keeping warm was a problem and there was no way I could use an electric fire all the time. I bought a paraffin heater and carried the paraffin up from the ironmonger's down the road. It was quite heavy but that was the only way I could pay independently for heating my room. Coming back from the office on a cold winter's day was quite a problem. The small kitchen was ideal for me. There was a gas cooker and a small table at which I ate my meals. That was where

I taught myself to cook all sorts of things and I used to enjoy making jam which I often gave away as presents. But all that came later. At first I could drink only milk and to this day I have a picture in my mind's eye of two milk bottles on the table.

Of course, there were lots of unforeseen difficulties, which had to be tackled. First of all, it was very difficult to practise my oboe, because the noise is penetrating. Fortunately, Mrs Fraser and the young couple - there was a series of them over the thirteen and a half years I was there - were often out so I had to wait till I was alone and then get on with it.

Washing clothes was a difficult job. I had to do this in my tiny kitchen sink and then take the soaking wet garments in a basin down the eighteen steps from the back kitchen to the garden far below and into the wash-house, where there was an old-fashioned mangle. Then the clothes had to be hung up or put on a clothes-dryer until they were dry. It was not easy. People who knew these houses used to say to me, 'Don't tell me you go down there all by yourself in the dark. I couldn't.' I suppose it was just something I had to do. It never occurred to me to feel scared. Two things I had to buy immediately were an iron and an ironing--board. These were the days before drip-dry, non-iron garments.

I had to tell my employers that I had moved. Naturally, a change of address had to be noted by the firm. No comments were made either by them or by me.

After moving to Muirend I went to the nearest church the following Sunday. I had been a Church of Scotland member for several years by then. Netherlee Church was a lovely building and it was within easy walking distance. I asked to speak to the

Sunday School Superintendent as I wished to teach in the Senior Department. The following Sunday - my second time at the church - he sought me out and to my utter astonishment he asked me if I would like to be Secretary of the Sunday School. 'But,' I protested, 'you don't know me and you don't know whether I would be any good or not'. 'That's true,' he replied, 'but we've never had anyone volunteering to teach in the Sunday School before, so we felt you must be interested'. I accepted the invitation and was in the job for the next ten years, during which time there were only two Superintendents. It was a huge Sunday School with 400 children and several departments, all fully staffed. I helped to run Parents' Nights and I organised several annual week-end conferences for the teachers. These were held at different venues and the guest speakers I had invited contributed much to their success. Those were the days when I went to church at 11am, Sunday School in the afternoon and then church at 6.30pm. I was devoted to Netherlee Church. I made many lovely friends there, especially the folk who sat in or near my pew.

The Minister was the Rev Stanley Mair, a splendid preacher and a most colourful character, who was always in great demand as a speaker. His father had been a missionary in China and Stanley went to Fordyce Academy and Aberdeen University, where he met and married a local minister's daughter, Isobel Caldwell. During World War II he was one of Orde Wingate's Chindits. Stanley served Netherlee Church with distinction for thirty years. HIs old car made such a noise when it started that he used to say that was why he was called 'the Rev'!

Stanley's wife, Isobel, became a doctor. Her particular interest was in handicapped children, culminating in the creation of the Isobel Mair School in Williamwood. When she retired she was unstoppable and went to Thailand to see what could be done for handicapped children in the northern villages there. She was voted Scotswoman of the Year in 1990, having already been awarded the MBE. The Mairs had five sons, and Stanley said that the last one was to be called 'Nae' - an example of typical Stanley humour. He died in 1976 at the age of 64. What a tremendous force for good the Mairs were in the community.

Well, all this time life in digs went on. I had my job in Blackie's; I was involved in my musical activities; I visited my mother regularly, very often walking all the way there and back via Cathcart and I managed to have one or two holidays.

I went to Jersey, Guernsey, the Isles of Scilly and the Ring of Kerry before my first holiday abroad to Italy. I visited Florence, Siena, San Gimignano, Assisi and Rome.

My Italian was practically non-existent except for my knowledge of musical terms but I put -*izione* on to words and managed quite well. In Florence, I went to a concert of Vivaldi oboe music given by I Musici in the Palazzo Vecchio. I asked a policeman for directions so he took me there, deposited me on the steps and bowed low. (I could do with more of this, I thought!) On the way home I got the train in Rome for Milan. In the carriage were two Italian policemen. The one on my left was very quiet, reading his newspaper. The other, opposite me, had no English but that did not stop his chat. He was dying to talk to me and, having noticed the label on my case above, he said, 'Ah! Santa Caterina di Siena'. Periodically he would look out the window and say, 'Il sole, bene, bene, bene'. Finally, I plucked up courage and said to my quiet neighbour, 'Il vostro amico e troppo volubile' which produced gales of laughter while my chatty friend pointed at his wedding ring. 'Oh dear,' I thought, 'I've put my foot in it here'. So I asked a lady in the compartment what 'volubile' meant and she said, 'Ah, it means always changing'. I asked, 'Does it mean fickle?' and she replied, 'Ah yes, that's right'. I should have said 'Il vostro amico parla troppo.' (Your friend talks too much.) When we got to Milan the two policemen took my luggage and saw me on to the train for Paris. Felice ricordi!

Not long after I left home Dr Milne died very suddenly from a heart attack and for a short time I saw his successor, who also died suddenly from a heart attack. By this time, I was fortunately getting better, albeit slowly. I had managed to buy crockery and cutlery and was beginning to entertain a few visitors in a modest way.

My next ordeal was a gynaecological operation in Stobhill Hospital which turned out to be highly beneficial. I remember the consultant commenting on my speedy recovery but I cannot remember how long I was off work.

While I was in digs I became particularly friendly with a family who lived close by who were also in Netherlee Church. Jim was the Deputy Head of the Child Guidance Service in Glasgow and an elder, and his wife, Meta, was the kindest, most maternal soul you could imagine. Their son was doing his National Service but the daughter, much younger, was at home and sometimes I helped out by staying with her as she was too young to be left alone. They had noticed me coming and going and the friendship developed in such a way that I was expected for high tea every Sunday. They were absolutely wonderful to me and I will never cease to be grateful to them for their superb kindness.

Mrs Fraser had a married daughter with one son and she went to stay with them in England for Christmas. The married couples all went off to be with relatives, so I was usually alone in the house over the Festive Season. Friends in the church would invite me for meals, so things were not entirely bleak. I always had the house looking spick and span for Mrs Fraser's return.

Towards the end of 1960 I developed a feeling of unease in Blackie's. I began to wonder if the firm was going to close down. And so began my tedious search for another job - a cue, perhaps, to start another chapter.

9 - William Collins Sons & Co Ltd

A great family business

It was rather a hopeless task to find another editorial post in Glasgow. All such jobs were in London and the competition would be severe. Also, I was totally unsuited to life in London and not fit for it either. I simply could not face it. The weeks went by and I decided to write to Hope Collins to ask if there was an opening there. He interviewed me and offered me a job in their Educational Department, which I believe he was keen to develop, but he refused to put up my miserable salary by even a small amount. In April 1961 I reluctantly said farewell to my colleagues in Blackie's and started in Collins. The Senior Art Editor in Blackie's had already gone to a post there.

The firm occupied a huge building on the north side of Cathedral Street. A new building had been constructed further along to act as a book store with a canteen on the top floor. There, 'minestone soup, rossitti and gateux' were regularly on the menu. The canteen staff had problems spelling! Latterly, I used to meet Kathleen Blackie at lunch. She was one of the daughters of Walter Graham Blackie, the Chairman in my day there, and it was thought to be strange that a member of the Blackie family was an employee of Collins. Kathleen was a geography graduate and was in the Atlas Department. Maybe she had inherited her father's love of atlases! The huge building in Cathedral Street has long since gone and the book store and canteen building became part of the University of Strathclyde.

The reception I got in the Educational Department was very far from promising. My new colleagues more or less ignored me and - can you believe it? - I was not even given a desk or table of my own. I had to do my work as best I could with galley proofs falling off the edge of someone else's desk. It was extraordinary that anyone was expected to tolerate such a situation and I did not intend to for long. One day, when walking along our corridor, I noticed a completely unused desk in one of the other rooms. I spoke to the Educational Manager about it, suggesting that, if it were at all possible, it be moved along for my use. That was what happened. It was not exactly an auspicious beginning. My few male colleagues were not graduates and had worked their way up from the factory floor, as far as I could see. They probably resented me and were just not prepared to give me a welcome, which was unfortunate. Eventually things changed and another graduate editor was engaged. Peter and I shared an office latterly and, while we could scarcely be described as bosom pals, he and I rubbed along together well enough. I remember a very strange episode when our offices were being radically altered and we had to get out of the way. Peter and I were temporarily relocated in the Directors' corridor no less! The Directors had their own dining-room there and their cook produced the meals in her own little kitchen nearby. She was a nice, friendly lady and Peter and I used to get lots of lovely leftovers from her, which we thoroughly enjoyed.

When our new offices were ready, Peter and I shared a large room. At one point we were joined by an editorial assistant called Monica Foot. She was the wife of Paul Foot, the nephew of Michael Foot, the well-known politician. I have no idea why she was even in Glasgow but there she was and Peter and I just had to accept the situation. Very soon she started to stir up trouble with the employees and, while I cannot now remember the details, I think it had something to do with unions. I found it very upsetting because of being in the same room and thinking I might be accused of unacceptable behaviour. Of course I had no desire to be involved. It was not long before she was dismissed on the spot.

In the spring of 1964 we had a trainee called Anthony Atha, who was related in some way to the Collins family. He was a typical Londoner trying (not very enthusiastically) to fit into the Glasgow scene. He was likeable but he drove us mad with his constant chatter and did not do a stroke of work. Here is the poem I made up about him. It was published in *Fontana* magazine.

To a Trainee

There was a young laddie called Tony,
Whose accent was really quite phoney.
'Haud yer wheesht' he would say
In Harrovian way,
And he lived in a cot all aloney.

Now Tony was fond of the shootin',
And at weekends he always was scootin'
Awa' in his car,
Where the bonnie deer are,
Wi' his guns, and his noisy horn hootin'.

Now Tony was usually pleasant,
Though his chatter was almost incessant.
You can see by his eye
He eats too much game pie.
He's beginning to look like a pheasant!

Now Tony was fond of the cookin',
And his roving eye always was lookin'
For recipes new,
To try out on - who?
For we never knew who he was hookin'!

Now Tony was fond of the lassies;
He hails every bright thing that passes,
Saying, 'By Jove, I fear
There's no pretty girls here,
But in London there's masses and masses.'

Now, Tony, please don't be offended.
Your humour is highly commended;
But if you insist
On doing the Twist
In a place where it isn't intended

Then, Tony you'll have to be scolded
For you shouldn't require to be tolded
This isn't the place
For choreographic grace,
And to our ways you'll have to be moulded.

Haud yer wheesht, man, and stop all this riot.
Dear Anthony, why don't you try it?
PLEASE,
get off to D*
And leave us at C**
Enjoying some nice peace and QUIET!

(* Reference Books
** Educational
Department)

As an obligement to the Directors, Peter and I used to mark the exam papers set annually for the admission of new apprentices. To become an apprentice in Collins was something that was very much sought after in those days. The exam papers consisted of several general knowledge questions, some simple arithmetic, and an essay on 'What I would do with £1,000'. The sort of answers we got were along the lines of:

'How many legs has an insect?' 'It depends.'

Ben Lomond was constantly being confused with Mount Everest and given some ridiculous heights. The essays were usually just a few sentences, such as - 'I would give some of it to my granny' - which used to make me warm to the candidate - but only momentarily - because most of the time it was a hard job to give the candidates any marks at all. But we had many a laugh.

Each year a Burns Supper was held in Collins. This function was open to all, from Directors and their wives down to the lowliest of employees. In 1965 I was asked to give the reply to the Toast to the Lasses which was going to be proposed by Alan Macfarlane of B Department. The Immortal Memory was proposed by the Rev Dr William Barclay, Professor of New Testament at Trinity College, Glasgow, and an eminent figure in the Church of Scotland. He had an office in Collins' premises as he was much involved in writing a series called *The Plain Man's Guides*.

That night I was at the top table between Mr Ian Collins, the brother of the Chairman, Sir William, and Mr Hope Collins, his cousin, who was my Director. He was the Chairman for the evening. During the course of the evening, Mr Ian and I realised that we were getting colder and colder as a heater nearby was not functioning properly. He very kindly asked if he could get my coat for me. I said that would be fine but warned him that it was a tatty old fur coat and not to be confused with a mink owned by a Director's wife. He brought me a large, hefty pullover of his, which he put over my knees! Professor Barclay gave a splendid Immortal Memory, as you would expect. He lived near Cathcart Railway Bridge and very kindly drove me home to Muirend - a bit further along the Clarkston Road. So it was a memorable night for me. My speech was published in full in *Fontana* magazine. There is no point in reproducing it here as it was a speech composed very much for the occasion with humorous references to various Collins characters, the Directors, and what was going on in Collins at the time.

Some years later I was at another Collins Burns Supper, which was memorable for a very different reason. The department had changed a lot. The Manager had died prematurely and we had a new Director, Leslie Murby, who came from Nelson's and brought with him a Senior Editor and an Art Editor as well as his secretary. I now had a room to myself with my name on it and my title was 'Senior Production Editor'. At the Burns Supper I am thinking of, Bill, our Senior Editor, had been asked to propose the Immortal Memory and was given a time limit of twenty minutes for his talk. Bill was an exceedingly pedantic and boring individual. He was not terribly popular. I felt I could get nowhere with him. That night his speech lasted at least forty minutes. We were all bored to tears and those who really understood what he was talking about would be in the minority and I was not one of them. Next day, in the Ladies', a colleague met one of the cleaners who said, 'Oh my, wasn't Mr M. just marvellous last night. I couldnae unnerstaun' a word of it. He's a real erudity man!'

10 - Teething Troubles and a New Challenge

'Sans teeth', but definitely not sans everything (sorry, Shakespeare!)

It was some time in 1965 that I decided to have all my teeth out. I had suffered a great deal with my teeth for most of my life and I felt I simply had to face up to the problem. When I awoke from the gas I found I was left with one tooth on the top left, and some on the bottom left and a crack into the sinus on the right. No action whatsoever was taken by the dentist and no apology was given. I suppose I must have gone back to Muirend by taxi. I felt very ill and I remember coming downstairs, clutching at the bannisters to speak to Mrs Fraser. I had to get to the Dental Hospital right away and Mrs Fraser insisted on coming with me. The surgeon there was appalled at the mess that had been made of me. I was operated on right away, sitting up with a local anaesthetic. My mouth was slit inside, to enable bits of bone to be removed and then stitched up. There were several students standing around and after the operation the surgeon asked them what they should do now with me. Since there was no answer forthcoming, I mumbled as best I could, 'Put her onto antibiotics,' which caused surprise and amusement. When I expressed concern about my remaining teeth, the surgeon said I would have them surgically removed at the hospital, but I had to wait until I could chew on the side that had been operated on.

Thereafter I spent ages in bed, feeling very ill and when my GP heard about it he immediately doubled the dose of penicillin, as he was afraid of an infection developing. Fortunately, that did not happen. I recovered and had to go back to work, looking a pretty sorry sight. I remember wondering why a woman in the bus was staring at me so much. I had momentarily forgotten the mess I was in, you see. I do not now remember how long I had to wait before I could have my remaining teeth out but eventually it happened and that, of course, was nothing like as traumatic as the previous operation. So there I was completely toothless. This was a terrible disaster for an oboist, of course.

Although, as I said, I was at my work, I realised that I would certainly not be out and about during the evenings so I decided to take up Modern Greek. Having Classical Greek already, I was very much interested in it. I put an advert into the paper under the 'Wanted Column'. I got a reply very quickly from a young Greek chap called Aneévas Zafeériathes. (I have transliterated his name to help the reader to pronounce it.) He came to see me and I explained to him the unfortunate situation I was in, adding that I wanted to put the time at my disposal to good use. He was a very nice young man, who was mad keen to work in a hotel, preferably for Reo Stakis, the Greek hotelier who was much to the fore in Glasgow then. I got on well with Aneévas and my weekly lessons. He promised me that, when I got my teeth, he would take me in his car to the Central Hotel for afternoon tea.

I have no idea now what I paid for the lessons but they must have been affordable. I decided I would like to give Aneévas something, as he was so kind to me. I had made some lemon curd so I gave him a big jar of it. Later on I asked him how he had liked it. 'Ah, zee lemon. I go like zees,' and he indicated that he had supped it. Concealing my astonishment, I said to him, 'Well, I wonder if you know this expression, but you must have a sweet tooth.' He replied, 'I have tirty-two sweet teeth!' (And I did not have even one!)

The day came when I was to get my dentures. They did not fit, so I was faced with a further wait. I did not see again the dentist who had made such a mess of me. I expect he could not face me. I was palmed off on to his dentist brother. They were lucky they got off with it all. Eventually I got my dentures and Aneévas took me to the Central Hotel as promised. I said goodbye to him and I learned later that he had indeed got a job in one of Reo Stakis's hotels.

Since the dentures were nothing special, I was strongly advised to go to a posh dental practice in Glasgow and be prepared to pay for expert attention. That was a great improvement and I am still registered with that practice. I did play the oboe again but it was just not the same. Many other denture-wearers told me that they did not know they had them but I never had the pleasure of reaching that stage.

Armed with my little knowledge of Modern Greek, I went to the Extramural class at Glasgow University for the next two years, after which I asked the lecturer (who was a Greek) if he could recommend some way in which I could progress with it, as there were no more classes available. He said he would make enquiries among the Greek students at the University. I was soon put in touch with Alekos and Mimeka Kakavoulis and that was the start of a friendship that continues to this day. They were in digs with Miss Margaret Stewart, a remarkable lady who had been deaf for most of her life. In spite of her disability she had been a well-known Church of Scotland missionary in Jamaica. She lived near the University, within walking distance for Alekos. He was studying for his MEd degree and I helped him with his English in his thesis, which was on St Basil. I sometimes had difficulty with his writing and I came across what I thought was 'St Basil taught his monks to make love' but 'love' was in fact 'shoes'. What a laugh we had about that - a laugh that was repeated for many years! Mimeka was a Primary School teacher in Greece and she it was who was able to continue my lessons in Modern Greek once a week. Their first child was born in Glasgow and we used to joke about him being a Scot.

Alekos and Mimeka were a most charming couple and I got on famously with them. After Alekos's graduation they returned home to Athens. Alekos became Professor of Education in the University of Crete, while retaining their home in Athens. Occasionally they came back to Glasgow for a conference and I had the pleasure of seeing them again and showing them a little bit more of Scotland.

I remember saying to a Greek friend of theirs how difficult I found Modern Greek. Her reply was, 'snaw deefeecult'.

11 - Collins Again

Part of a large family

As I mentioned, the situation in the Educational Department had changed a great deal with new personnel brought in by our new Director, Mr Leslie Murby. If I could not make it with Bill, the Senior Editor, it was a different story with Mr Murby. Our department had about six representatives who covered the whole country, selling to schools and keeping an eye open for new authors and ideas. These Reps were amazing men in many ways and they all lived into their nineties. About twice a year they came from England for meetings in Glasgow and we always went out for a special lunch. Mr Murby lived in a top flat in Ramsay Garden, next to the Esplanade of Edinburgh Castle. There were seventy-five steps up to it and no lift. After the meetings we were invited there for a drinks party and the poor Reps used to hate it because all they wanted to do was get home. Of course, Mr Murby meant it all kindly, I am sure.

In his wisdom he decided that I was to accompany each Rep in turn and so, over many weeks at intervals, I spent a week with each of them, going round their areas. It was, I suppose, good experience for me but I do not know what the poor Reps were thinking! I kept up with the Leeds Rep until he died at the age of ninety-three. He was a bachelor and we were always wondering what headmistress he was charming next. It was a constant source of amusement to the other Reps. Another Rep I was friendly with was an excellent musician, so I had a lot in common with him. He had a brilliant sense of humour and I had a hilarious correspondence with him during the last few years of his life until he died at the age of ninety-five.

It is difficult to remember all the books I handled, as they were so numerous over the years and probably not of great general interest. However, there was one series which was memorable as it met with phenomenal success. It was a four-book English course for Primary Schools called *Using our Language* by a Primary School Headmaster, Mr Darley, who was based in Sheffield.

One day, very unexpectedly, Mr Murby said he wanted to meet Mr Darley and take me with him. Quite honestly, I do not know why he did but in due course it was all arranged. In those days I was virtually never in a car and indeed Mr Murby's drive to Sheffield was my first experience of a motorway. This all took place on 1st July 1969. We stayed at the Hallam Towers, which at that time was a very new hotel. When we arrived there, we noticed a very posh car parked nearby and I surprised Mr Murby by telling him it was an E-type Jaguar.

We got settled into our rooms and very soon Mr Murby was on the telephone, inviting me to his room to watch the Prince of Wales's Investiture on the television. At dinner that night he insisted on my having crêpes suzettes but I was not at all impressed. The next day we went to see Mr Darley but I do not now remember much about the visit except that Mr Darley was always wanting me to go and stay with him and his wife. This was hardly an invitation that I could accept very easily. Later on, when I was about to leave Collins, Mr Darley broke off his association with the firm and said that Collins was not the same without me.

We broke our return journey in Peebles, where Mr Murby and his Norwegian wife shared an estate called Hallyards with someone else. (Some of us used to refer to it as Hellyards, rather cheekily.) There was a statue of the Black Dwarf in the grounds and, quite frankly, I found it rather an eerie place. Mrs Murby gave us a lovely dinner and next day we drove back to Glasgow.

I often wondered what the rest of the staff thought about all that!

12 - A Friendly Footing

An expression used by Charles Lamb

I was always keen to get married but I never met anyone and it seemed very unlikely that I ever would. The years were rolling by. It must have been in 1967 or thereabouts that I decided to register with Heather Jenner's Marriage Agency. I was duly summoned for an interview and I had to go through to Edinburgh to her very large house one day for this purpose. I remember the visit clearly, but thereafter I was put in touch with a series of most unsuitable men, who lived too far away to get to know. I wrote to Mrs Jenner and complained bitterly. The next communication I had from her put me in touch with a chap called Iain, who lived a few miles further out of town in a country area called Waterfoot - surprisingly near, in fact. I got in touch with him and we met at the local shops, as I did not want him to come to my digs. We had dinner in a hotel in East Kilbride and afterwards, much to my dismay, Iain said to me, 'Well, I don't think we have much in common so maybe we should not continue to meet,' but I replied that we should not give up like that. He was a quiet, reserved sort of person and I could see that it would take some time to get to know him. So, that's how it all started and I have never told anyone that before! We agreed later that we would say we met in the train from Muirend into town, as Iain used to leave his car near the station there.

Our courtship was a very douce, slow affair.

> '*A fine romance, my dear, this is,*
> *A fine romance, with no kisses.*'

If you thought this was going to be me swept off my feet in a whirlwind, you are very much mistaken.

It might be helpful at this stage to tell you something about Iain's background. He was born and brought up in Pollokshields, a nice residential area on the south side of Glasgow. His father had died of a heart attack at the age of fifty-three and his mother had been a widow for many years. They also had a daughter a few years older than Iain. She became a GP and went to a practice in England, settling eventually in Birmingham after marrying a manufacturing jeweller.

Iain went to the local Primary School and then to the High School of Glasgow, which in those days was boys only and located in Elmbank Street in the city. He did his National Service in the Royal Engineers and was in Kuala Lumpur, which he greatly enjoyed. He was so thin that his nickname was Beanpole. He started business life in a firm of plumbers' merchants in town but transferred to another similar firm near the south end of the Kingston Bridge, eventually becoming a Director. From there it was very easy for him to go to his mother's flat in Nithsdale Road for his lunch, which he did most days. However, he had his own flat in Waterfoot, which is roughly halfway between Clarkston and Eaglesham, so he was well used to being on his own and cooking for himself. The flat was in a very pleasant position, well off the main road with the White Cart flowing nearby.

Iain's mother was a delightful lady but, even when I first came on the scene, she was becoming rather muddled. However, she was not too bad and was still able to live alone. She had a lovely sister, Aunt Agnes, who was married to Dugald, who had a most attractive humorous outlook on life. They lived in Bromsgrove in Kent.

As I have mentioned before, I was unused to being in a car. I went everywhere by public transport and thought nothing of it. Iain had started to drive at the age of seventeen and he was a very keen and capable driver with a great interest in cars. He had a little navy blue Spitfire which we used a lot. Some of his interest in cars began to rub off on to me, inevitably, and one day, feeling particularly smart, I said to him, 'Don't you think I'm getting very good at recognising the different models of cars?' His answer was, 'Oh, you're just at the stage of a seven-year-old boy'.

Our friendship did develop, albeit at a snail's pace. I would have married Iain after six months, but I had to wait for another long year. One lovely day we were at Neidpath Castle, sitting on a bench beside the Tweed. 'Ah,' I said to myself, 'this is the moment he is going to go down on bended knee and beg for my hand in marriage.' (Not blooming likely.) It was always a great disappointment to me that we did not go on holiday together - at least, not at that time - because that is a good way to get to know somebody. Latterly, I began to wonder if each outing was going to be the last, but then I always was such a worrier. (Iain used to say that there was nothing I could not worry about, if I put my mind to it!)

Fooling about in a photo booth

Iain had always been keen on dancing and one day he asked me if I would like to go to dancing lessons. Things were looking up! I said I'd love it. So we went to private lessons in Ballroom and Latin American dancing at Roger McEwan's, a well-known Dance School off Sauchiehall Street. Our charming teacher, Eileen Stewart, gave us a weekly lesson, which we much enjoyed. And so began our long love-affair with dancing.

All this time, of course, I was working in Collins but my colleagues knew nothing about my personal life. We always took our main holiday in July and in 1969 we had arranged a holiday together in Menorca. You may recall that on 1st July 1969 I had been in Sheffield with my Director, Mr Murby. Shortly after that Iain and

I went out for the evening and came back to my digs. I was standing pouring the tea, when Iain suddenly said, 'I think we should get married'. I got such a shock I nearly dropped the teapot! When I got back to Collins I sought an interview with Mr Murby and told him I was engaged to be married. Considering I had been at pains to keep my relationship private, his utter amazement could not be concealed but he was, of course, delighted.

Seeing we had the holiday in Menorca arranged, we decided to let that stand. We enjoyed our two weeks there but we found the island very undeveloped with very rough roads. We hired a small car. Iain was very keen on boats and, if there was water about, he was always wanting to be on it, if at all possible. We were on a beach one day and there were pedalos for hire. Ours had no rudder so that was no good. What a strange thing the brain is! To this day I remember how I worked out the Spanish for 'Where is the rudder?' *Dond' esta el timon*? - and got one from the office!

There was absolutely no point in delaying the wedding so we fixed it for 19th September 1969 and decided on a brief weekend honeymoon.

And that was our 'friendly footing before marriage'.

WM. COLLINS SONS & CO. LTD.

Publishers · Manufacturing Stationers

144, CATHEDRAL ST. GLASGOW. C.4.

Telephone: Bell 4031
Telegrams: "Collins Glasgow"

Chairman
W. A. R. Collins

Monday

Just a very short note to send you both our very best wishes for Friday. We are all so happy you are going to share on with us. Again all good luck and every happiness for the future.

Ian Collins

So sorry I am away this week and so I can't see you before Friday.

Mr Ian Collins's letter on the occasion of my marriage

13 - My Move to Waterfoot

'Come live with me and be my love' (John Donne)

When I left Mrs Fraser's house for the last time I had been there for thirteen and a half years. We were married on 19th September 1969 in Netherlee Church by the minister, the Rev Stanley Mair.

The signing session with the Rev Stanley Mair

Iain had joined the church earlier. I did not want to be a white bride. My outfit was a lovely silver grey dress and coat with a turquoise zig-zag pattern on it and I had a beautiful turquoise hat and silver grey accessories.

Leaving Netherlee Church after our wedding, 19th September 1969

There were about eleven invited guests, close relatives only. Since my father had died by this time, a second cousin of my mother, whom we called Uncle Bert, gave me away. I had no bridesmaids.

Jane arrived back from Bombay only the day before the wedding. She was as thin as a rake and had to be given one of my garments for the occasion. Lots of my Netherlee friends came to the service. Mr Murby, my Director in Collins, also came and we spoke to everyone at the church door. I had requested music of my own choice for the ceremony and we left the church to Widor's Toccata. William Liddell FRCO was our superb organist.

The reception was held in the Redhurst Hotel in Eastwoodmains Road. The minister chaired the proceedings, of course, and we had many samples of his pawky humour. The cake was decorated with two small models - a yacht for Iain and an oboe for me.

Iain chose the Clarkston car park as the best place to leave his car - a bigger model than the Spitfire! - and we escaped from the hotel in a taxi to the car park, where we changed into our own car and departed to the Trossachs Hotel for our honeymoon. We had a bedroom in one of the circular towers. It was a very wet weekend but not one I am likely to forget.

I had to pay for most of the wedding myself. The photographs were all black and white, as I was told by my mother that we could not afford colour!

Shortly after our wedding Jane was accepted as a novice in the Benedictine Abbey in Wales. A year later, some time in 1970, we got a telephone call to the flat from a friend to say that she had called on my mother and found her dead in her chair - at least, she was pretty sure she was dead. We rushed over to King's Park immediately and, sure enough, my mother was indeed dead in her chair in the lounge - a nice way to go. I looked at her - completely dry-eyed - and said to myself, 'You will never be able to hurt me again'.

It may seem a strange thing to say but my gratitude to God knew no bounds. I was spared what I always dreaded - death-bed scenes with complaints, accusations and recriminations. In her will, there was nothing whatsoever left to Jane and me. The house and its contents were left to another relative. It was speedily cleared and sold and the door was finally closed on what was to me simply a nightmare.

Not long after this I went into Collins and found that Mr Leslie Murby had died very suddenly the night before. He used to holiday in Spain a lot and he and his wife had just climbed the seventy-five steps to their flat in Ramsay Garden beside Edinburgh Castle Esplanade, when Mr Murby collapsed at the door. I was very shocked and sorry about it. The very last photograph of him was the one taken at our wedding and it was particularly good.

Mr Hope Collins had died three years before that, which was a terrible blow to the firm. He took a heart attack while driving towards Argyle Street. Fortunately, someone realised what was happening and had the sense to stop the traffic so that no one else was hurt.

I soon began to realise that it was a bit of a disaster to have no voice on the Board. As the months went by in 1971 I began to feel more and more unsettled. I was by no means the only person in the department feeling this way. It was, I think, quite a general feeling.

One day a secretary came into my office and said to me quite bluntly, 'Why don't you get another job? Other people are leaving'. Well, perhaps it was not such a problem for a secretary or an accountant, for example, but for an editor it was an entirely different matter. However, it started me thinking and I decided to write to the University of Strathclyde to enquire if there was any job available there in which my expertise might be of use. I got a telephone call immediately (I remember it was on a Thursday) asking me to come for an interview at the lunch-hour next day. That was so convenient as I did not need to ask for any time off.

I was interviewed by the Academic Registrar and the Secretary to Senate and offered a job right away, What I did not know (until I was retiring, some sixteen years later) was that they had been advertising - without much success - for an editorial assistant and when my letter came in they jumped to the conclusion that I had applied for the post, whereas I knew nothing about the advert. The Personnel Officer had thrown my letter down in front of the Secretary to Senate, saying 'There's your answer to prayer!' So the following Monday I put in my notice.

While Iain's flat had a lot going for it, it was during the early autumn of 1971 that we began to feel we would prefer to live in a house. So we started to look around and we soon discovered that a three-bedroom villa was for sale about a mile along the road nearer Clarkston. This was a solid, detached house, one of six similar houses set back from the main road in a private road parallel to it. There was a smallish garden at the front and the large back garden went right down to the White Cart. The outlook beyond the river was open with fields and a wood some distance away. It was very charming and attractive and we bought it and planned to move as soon as was convenient. The move in October coincided with the start of my new job at the University of Strathclyde so I made arrangements to allow myself a week off to cope with settling in.

Some months previously it had been suggested that I should learn to drive and so I began to have driving lessons. They were a nightmare to me. I loathed them but I persevered and Iain was a model of patience when it came to my practice sessions. I got a Triumph Herald and passed my test round about the time of our move. Learning to drive was one of the best things I ever did.

In Clarkston there was a very tricky car park above the shops and I said to Iain that, during my week off, I was going to discipline myself to master it. So off I went in my car one afternoon to carry out my plan but when I got to Busby I changed my mind and I stopped the car at the roadside and crossed over to the shops. Suddenly there was a tremendous explosion and I said to the shop assistant, 'Goodness, what on earth was that?' She replied, 'Oh, probably some car backfiring'. (No way, I thought.)

I left the shop and decided to walk down the hill towards Clarkston Toll and there a terrible sight met my eyes. The road was full of ambulances and cluttered up with other vehicles. Dr Isobel Mair, the minister's wife, was picking her way back to her surgery. She saw me and raised her eyes heavenwards with a look of utter despair. There had been a build-up of gas in the cellar beneath the shops, right beneath the car park. Twenty-one people died and a hundred were injured. Had I carried out my plan I would have been one of them. There was no way I was going to add to the severe congestion so I returned to my car and came home. The telephones began to buzz with distraught folk trying to get news of their relatives and friends. The lady next door had gone to Clarkston to get money for a holiday. She had been on the zebra crossing at the time and thereafter she had endless trouble with a foot which was always being operated on.

And that was the Clarkston Disaster of 21st October 1971.

14 - An Academic Atmosphere

'A University should be a place of light, of liberty and of learning'
(Benjamin Disraeli)

When I started at the University of Strathclyde I made up my mind that I would give service but I would not be subservient. I was aware of the fact that I would be dealing with very clever people and I was quite determined that I was not going to feel overwhelmed by better brains than mine.

My job was to edit and produce all the official University publications - the *Calendar*, a most important volume with all the degree regulations, a full list of staff and a few other bits of information; the *Prospectus* with information for would-be students; the *Postgraduate Booklets*, of which there were several; and the *University Diary*, a copy of which was given to each member of staff. Various other odds and ends came my way. It was hard work but I was used to working on my own. In the Royal College Building I had an office to myself, and this led eventually to its being used as a convenient place for folk to offload all sorts of troubles!

I soon got to grips with the job and seldom bothered anyone. I got on very well with my boss, Dr Martin Lowe, the Secretary to Senate. They were, after all, the Senate publications and I had to develop quickly the skill of knowing what bits of information in the Senate Minutes affected the publications. I could see that my boss was the kind of person who did not like to be bothered with tiresome queries. Gradually I had to get to know my colleagues in the University Administration, of which I was on the fringe but not exactly a part. The Registrar was the Head with the Academic

Registrar, the Secretary to Court and the Secretary to Senate next in line. There were Clerks to the Faculties, who were responsible for the relevant student administration.

I very soon realised that things seldom stayed the same. Degree regulations changed and there were additional new degrees; staff members changed all the time and so did their qualifications. The University was very new, having been founded in 1964. Having joined the staff in October 1971, I had to devise ways of keeping track of these changes and develop my own filing systems. This in itself caused a great deal of work.

After only a short time in the job I had a call from one of the Professors of Architecture. He asked to see me, as he wanted to make changes to the department's *Postgraduate Booklet*. So off I went to his office. Professor Morcos Asaad was an Egyptian, on the plump side, with a twinkle in his eye. After he had dealt with the main alterations he said, 'Meesees Leeston, could you please put in a couple of new qualifications for me?' 'Certainly, Professor,' I replied, but I added, mischievously, 'but you do realise that you will now take up two lines?' 'Meeses Leeston, look at me. Don't you think I deserve to take up two lines?' After that, we were always the best of pals.

It must be remembered that this was long before the days of computers, although on the printing front there were slight rumblings of change. Dealing with printers and their representatives was another important part of my job. Obviously, I could give work to only a certain number of firms but I tried to be kind and sympathetic to these men, who were after all only doing their best to get business for their firms in a highly competitive market. I got to know some of them quite well.

There was one chap, who had the most attractive accent and there was something very likeable about him. He came from the Isle of Lewis and his father had been a tram-driver in Glasgow. One day he said to me, 'I have got a cow'. I had to do some quick thinking and pull myself together, while stifling a smile. 'Really, how interesting!' I blurted out. At his next visit, he said to me, 'Would you like to see the cow?' I replied, 'That would be very nice but it would also be good to meet your wife'. That led to a long friendship with his family. He used to tell me that he was terrified of my opposite number in Glasgow University and could hardly bring himself to knock on her door. I said that surely it couldn't be as bad as that but he insisted that it was!

I built up a great relationship with David J Clark, the printers. It was David J Clark Junior who called on me and I gave them a lot of business. David was a charming, friendly, humorous young man and it was always a pleasure to see him. However, I was very tough on the firm and would not tolerate mistakes, so much so that David devised a series of graded imaginary punishments for the offending members of his staff, such as thumbscrews, for example. The worst thing was an execution in Cadogan Street! I also insisted on having things done on time and for the most part, with my bossy ways, I achieved this. If you can do business and have some fun, how much nicer it is!

David and I were both very keen on cats. He had a cat called Rover. At one point, I was 'between cats' and David said he'd be able to get me a kitten easily enough as there were always litters on farms near his home. The weeks passed, however, and there was no kitten. One morning, when I was at my desk, I heard a miaow, so, thinking it was a cat stuck on a ledge outside, I got up to investigate. Then I saw David at the door with his hand round it, holding a black kitten. 'You've been without a cat long enough,' he said, 'so I got this one for you from the Cat and Dog Home'. The wee kitten sat in the pending tray, looking at me with topaz eyes, so I called her Topaz. It was a bit of a problem for me, though. I said to David, 'What a risk you have taken. I might not have been going home tonight straight from the office and then what?' He said he would just have taken the kitten home himself. Topaz was amazingly good all day and I arranged with Iain to pick me up outside the building. I did not have anything to put her in, but we got home safely with my new furry friend. Later on David handed me the receipt for 50p from the Cat and Dog Home, saying that it was Topaz's birth certificate!

The University of Strathclyde was founded in 1964 when the Royal College of Science and Technology ('the Tech') amalgamated with the Scottish College of Commerce. The first Chancellor was Lord Todd, a huge man known as Lord God and the first Principal was Sir Samuel Curran. Lord Todd was a daunting figure and so was Lady Todd, whom I met occasionally at our annual Commemoration Day, when distinguished persons were awarded honorary degrees. On these occasions my job was to look after the VIPs and/or their spouses. For the most part they were very pleasant but now and then I had to cope with someone who was standoffish.

Commemoration Day, April 1978 – with the then Lord Provost of Glasgow, David Hodge, and 'his man'. Lady Curran is in the background.

One day, out of the blue, I was told that Sir Samuel Curran insisted on having me attend his private dinner to look after the VIPs. I found this very strange because I was surprised that Sir Sam even knew I existed. This was a very pleasant occasion with Helen McArthur as the guest singer. Apparently the Principal held an annual dinner to show appreciation to those he wished to thank.

Professor Richard Rose, a Professor of Politics, who had set up the Centre for the Study of Public Policy in the University and who was one of the most prolific writers I have ever come across, asked me to do private editorial work for him. I cannot now remember how it all started but this led to a lengthy involvement with very detailed proof-reading of statistical tables, besides other texts. Sometimes I made up indexes as well. It was scarcely a bundle of fun and I was paid peanuts. One day I actually said to Professor Rose, 'You know, I pay my gardener more per hour than you pay me.' I do not remember a dramatic improvement but I suppose it says something for me that there were never any mistakes in his vast tomes and he always acknowledged my involvement very kindly in the Prefaces. He was American with a strong accent and he inspired in me a very strange feeling of loyalty. I did a lot of work for him and when I retired he wrote a very charming letter to me saying how sorry he was not to be at my farewell but that when he thought of my work the expression 'Clyde- Built' came to mind. Coming from him, it was something I valued a great deal.

In 1982 I began to get involved with the Women's Club in the University but that deserves a chapter to itself.

15 - The Monstrous Regiment

A bit daunting, I must say

There was a Women's Club in the University. As I was never very keen on females en masse, I joined the Club in a sort of half-hearted way but, as it turned out, I became very involved in it, so much so that I feel it deserves a chapter to itself.

Membership was open to any female employee of the University and wives of academics. The Club offered friendship to the wives of overseas students, who were often lonely, and for that I admired it greatly. They really did a great job there. We had evening meetings with speakers. On one such occasion we had Sheriff Irvine Smith. He was a formidable character in the court and I admired him greatly. I was much amused when Lady Curran said to me that during his speech she had been terrified of him!

We also had most interesting evening visits to some of the University Departments, such as the Bioengineering Unit and the Scottish Hotel School when it was based at Ross Hall in Crookston. Thirdly, we had lunch talks. I think it must have been about 1981 that I was asked to take charge of them and I did this for twenty-four years. I spent a lot of time doing votes of thanks because no one else would do them.

I was asked repeatedly to join the committee but I kept refusing, as I felt I already had enough to do. In 1984 I went to the AGM as usual and the outgoing Chairman begged me to go on the committee. In a moment of weakness, I gave in and said, 'Well, all right. I'll do a short stint'. To my amazement and horror - and without as much as a 'by your leave', my name was written on the blackboard against Vice-Chairman. To protest publicly would have been very unseemly, surely. When I became Chairman in 1985 I continued to organise the Lunch Talks.

The Lunch Talks were very popular. They took place on the second Tuesday of each month from October to May. I had many distinguished speakers, several of whom went on to become even more distinguished. I remember Lady Williams telling us in 1984 what it was like to be the wife of the Principal of Glasgow University, Sir Alwyn Williams. She was a most charming person. One day I met her in Jenners' in Edinburgh and we lunched together before going on to our meetings.

The Very Rev Dr Andrew Herron, formerly Clerk to the Presbytery of Glasgow and a former Moderator of the General Assembly of the Church of Scotland, entertained us hugely with his humorous reminiscences. In 1987 I invited Joyce Deans to speak to us as she had become the first woman President of the Glasgow Institute of Architects. In 1988 we had Elizabeth Roads, former secretary to the Lord Lyon, who had become in 1986 Lyon Clerk and Keeper of the Records at the Court of the Lord Lyon in Edinburgh - her appointment being the first time in its 400-year history that the Lyon Court has had a woman in one of its senior positions. At the time of her talk she had just acquired a son and I referred to him as the 'Lyon cub'!

In April 1989, the Rev Lorna Hood spoke on 'Women and God'. She had been minister of Renfrew North Parish Church for nine years at a time when there were few women ministers. She later became Moderator of the General Assembly of the Church of Scotland and now she is the Very Rev Dr Lorna Hood.

The session 1988-89 was the last one of the Women's Club, which sadly had to close down because of lack of support of the evening meetings. The Lunch Talks came under the aegis of the Staff Club, which was pleased to have them, so I continued to run them for twenty-four years in all, during which time we had 168 distinguished speakers.

It was a very special pleasure and privilege to have Lady Marion Fraser, the wife of Sir William Kerr Fraser, a former Principal and Vice-Chancellor of the University of Glasgow, to talk to us about being Her Majesty's Lord High Commissioner to the General Assembly of the Church of Scotland in both 1994 and 1995. This most charming lady gave us a fascinating picture of what went on behind the scenes. I remember her saying she had to buy so many new clothes for these occasions that she felt she would never need to buy any more. She later became a Lady of the Thistle, a personal gift of HM The Queen, for her services.

In March 1997 a vast audience turned out to hear Heather Reid, a weather forecaster based at the Glasgow Weather Centre and frequently on TV. She was affectionately known as 'Heather the Weather'.

In February 1998 we had a most unusual speaker and I forget now how I got to know him. Robert Morris, the Joint Managing Director of the Morris Furniture Company, was a most likeable character with his frizzy fair hair and his jeans. In the past the company made furniture for many famous liners and hotels. He was highly entertaining - indeed, Lady Curran telephoned me to say how much she had enjoyed his talk - and he insisted on our visiting the factory in Castlemilk, which we did. There we were treated like VIPs and we all got a mug which says on it 'Stolen from the Morris Café'. I still have mine. Since those days I have met Robert Morris once or twice.

Another eminent and memorable speaker, loaded with degrees, was Gavin Arneil, Emeritus Professor of Child Health in the University of Glasgow, whom I knew personally. In 1983 he had been awarded the St Mungo Prize for his work on clearing up rickets in Glasgow. He came in November 1999 to speak on 'Health for the World's Children'. At that time, he was the immediate Past President of the International Pediatric (sic) Association. Iain and I used to meet the Arneils quite often in Glasgow Airport, when they were going about the Association's business. Everywhere he went he was fêted of course, with special meals, for example, which were not always to his liking. On one occasion he noticed a small hammer beside the cutlery. He asked what this was for and was told he would soon see. Something live and moving was served and had to be dealt a blow with the hammer. There was no way Professor Arneil was going to eat that. It gave him the creeps. On another occasion there was a whole roast pig and he was presented with the delicacy par excellence - the ears - a couple of leathery objects with bristly hairs. It was enough to make him long for mince and tatties!

In February 2001 we had a talk from Hamish G Hardie about the recovery and restoration of the Tall Ship, the *Glenlee*. He was Chairman of the committee responsible for this and his foresight and determination played a major role in bringing the ship back home from Seville to the River Clyde and in helping to solve the many problems during the restoration. Hamish Hardie, who was a Trustee and Vice-Chairman of the Clyde Maritime Trust, had been made an Honorary Doctor of the University of Strathclyde in November 1999. When the University celebrated its bicentenary in 1996, it chose the *Glenlee* to feature on its armorial bearings. The *Glenlee* is now moored beside the Riverside Museum of Transport.

On 12th March 2002 Sheriff David Buchanan Smith of North Strathclyde at Kilmarnock spoke to us about his great passion - curling. In 1981 he had published a book about it entitled *Curling: An Illustrated History*. He was Secretary and Treasurer of the Scottish Curling Museum Trust and was President of the Curling Clubs of both Ayr and Symington and was also President of the Eglinton County Curling Game, instituted by the Earl of Eglinton in 1851. What was so appropriate about his talk was that the Ladies Scottish Curling Team had just won gold medals in the Olympics and everyone thought that the talk had been arranged because of that but, of course, the talk had been arranged many months before and it was all just a very happy coincidence.

In November 2002 we had a special talk for the Queen's Golden Jubilee year from the Rev James M Gibson, Minister of Bothwell Parish Church. He told us about his unexpected invitation to Balmoral. His talk was highly entertaining but admirably discreet as well.

In February 2005 Dr Mona Siddiqui, as she was then, spoke to us about Islam. I have always admired her tremendously. A person of formidable intellect, she was at that time Head of the Department of Theology and Religious Studies and Senior Lecturer in Arabic and Islamic Studies in the University of Glasgow. She was also much involved with the BBC as a broadcaster and consultant on issues of Islam. For some time now she has been Professor Siddiqui and she has moved to the University of Edinburgh.

Sadly, session 2005 to 2006 had to be the final one for the Lunch Talks as the Staff Club had to close, like so many similar clubs, due to lack of support. In November 2005 I was pleased to welcome Professor Jim McDonald to speak to us on 'Future Energy Systems'. He joined the University of Strathclyde in 1984, ultimately becoming Rolls-Royce Professor of Electrical Power Systems in 1994. In 2005 he was Head of the Department of Electronic and Electrical Engineering and in 2009 he became Principal of the University of Strathclyde.

The talk in December 2005 could not have been more different. It was given by twins, John and Peter Douglas from Dumbarton, and that in itself was most unusual. They were retired cinema projectionists, who reminisced about their forty-four years in Glasgow cinemas and entertained us hugely. I called their talk 'Reel Reminiscences' and the twins spoke turn about in an amazingly seamless way. It was a memorable and unique experience.

The very last speaker was Francis J Meehan MA (Glas), MPA (Harvard), LLD (Glas) and the title of his talk was 'How I won the Cold War Single-Handed'. Dr Meehan specialised in Soviet-German affairs and in East and Central Europe. He was the US Ambassador to Czechoslovakia from 1979 to1980; to Poland from 1980 to 1983; and to East Germany from 1985 to 1988. So I think I can fairly say that my twenty-four years of Lunch Talks went out on a high.

I now organise two Reunion Lunches annually - one in the spring and one in the autumn - in the Western Club in Glasgow for those who attended the Lunch Talks and were so disappointed when they had to stop. These lunches are very much appreciated and at least we still keep in touch.

16 - The Social Whirl

I never expected to be in it

Iain and I were ideally suited. Neither of us was the least bit interested in sport of any kind. We were a great team. We did everything together. I livened him up and he calmed me down. He was definitely the meat in my sandwich.

We settled down to life in our new house. We liked it very much. It was very private and we often had the company of a heron in the White Cart at the foot of the garden. We seldom saw our neighbours as we were all out at business. The cat next door chose to live with us, escaping from a house with young children and a labrador. Fortunately, the folks next door did not mind.

My mother-in-law was always referred to as Mother Liston. As I have already mentioned, she was becoming rather muddled and her condition was worsening. We heard that she had crossed the road to the baker's shop opposite her flat in Pollokshields, bought a big bag of buns and eaten them all in the street - not the sort of behaviour you would expect from a genteel lady! She had a voracious appetite. When she was having her high tea with us she would start eating the food on the plates before we had sat down, so I had to put it all on the table at the last minute.

The time came when she could not live alone and we wondered what we should do. Not so far away from Mother Liston's flat was a Church of Scotland Home for unmarried mothers. In those days, of course, these poor lassies were disapproved of, and they were glad to be offered accommodation in which they could keep their babies. So we employed an Australian girl with a baby to live with Mother Liston and this was a wonderful success, as the baby was much loved and proved to be such a source of delight. However, we had to give the girl a day off, so every Sunday we called for Mother Liston. At that time, we were still members of Netherlee Church, but we felt we had no option but to take Mother Liston to her own church in Pollokshields where she was known, and then to Waterfoot to spend the rest of the day with us. This pattern was adhered to for a long time. After a year or so, the girl went back to Australia with her baby but we employed another girl from the Home. Frances was much older, was a trained nurse, came from Dalbeattie, and had a wee boy called Jonathan, whom Mother Liston adored. So this, too, was a highly successful arrangement and the Sunday visits continued.

One day we had a surprise visit from a tall gentleman to invite us to Maxwell Mearns Castle Church but we had to explain politely that we were members of Netherlee Church and had no intention of leaving it.

Shortly after that we had Mother Liston with us one very dreich Sunday in November and Iain was wondering where we could go to entertain her a bit and fill in the time. He asked me if I would like to spectate at the East Kilbride baths. I said I'd rather go to the Eastwood baths, so that's where we went. We had just sat down in the spectators' gallery when I turned round and instantly recognised my school-friend, Betty, whom I had not seen for over twenty years. We had lost touch with each other since schooldays, as she had got married and had three children, one of whom was swimming in the baths. Her husband was a civil engineer and they had to move around to different places, depending on his job. It turned out they lived very near us in Newton Mearns and we were invited soon after to dinner. The door was opened by her husband - the tall gentleman who had called on us recently to invite us to his church! So that was the start of a long and happy association.

Our socialising with Iain's sister and brother-in-law settled down to our annual short visit to them and their annual short visit to us. In order to give Mother Liston's carers and ourselves a holiday she went to her daughter's and we did the exchange at Kendal which worked well. Inevitably the time came when Mother Liston needed twenty-four-hour care. I felt this was a matter for Iain and his sister to deal with, so Mother Liston went to a care home in Birmingham. We went to see her at the next available opportunity. She was unrecognisable. Her hair was untidy and shoulder-length. I cried my heart out. I do not know whether she knew us or not. Her death shortly afterwards was a blessed release.

At a theme night – Kings and Queens – as the King and Queen of Diamonds

In full Highland dress

Iain very often wore full Highland dress to the social events at the University of Strathclyde, such as the Admin Dinner Dances and the Staff Club Burns Suppers. I used to help a bit with the latter and I organised and chaired two of them. The Women's Club also held mixed social events. The first Principal, Sir Samuel Curran, was succeeded by Professor Graham Hills. He and his wife, Mary, were very sociable - Mary, in particular, being very much to the fore in the Women's Club.

The Hills were succeeded by Professor John and Dr Elinor Arbuthnott. I will never forget the lovely events that Elinor arranged. In those days, the University had volunteers who came to stuff envelopes for big distributions and she hosted an annual luncheon for them but she also invited, so kindly, one or two other ladies, such as the wives of the current Vice-Principals, for example, and she invited me as well. We had a reception in the Court/Senate Suite, where we also had a full lunch. Thereafter we went to the Principal's Penthouse Suite at the very top of the Livingstone Tower for coffee and we always had a group photograph taken. I went to several of these very delightful luncheons.

For some time Iain had been a life member of the Royal Scottish Automobile Club. He lunched with his friends there. They called themselves (rather modestly!) 'The Glorious Twelve' but so many men wanted to join the group that they had to change their name to 'The Glorious Twelve and Others Forby'. The Club premises in Blythswood Square were absolutely beautiful and we went to all the Dinner Dances there, very often in a large group with all of us in full evening dress. For me, these occasions were such a treat. It was indeed a very sad day when, many years later, the RSAC had to close down.

At another theme night – The Sea and Ships – as the Hebridean Princess with my 'port and starboard' earrings and Iain with his special 'flag' tie.

During all this time, of course, we ourselves did a lot of entertaining at home and had many invitations to dinner. I think it would be fair to say that we really were part of the Social Whirl.

17 - Ross Priory

About a very special place on Loch Lomondside
and the folk who performed there.

This beautiful mansion, situated on the south bank of Loch Lomond, near the village of Gartocharn, with unrivalled views of Ben Lomond, Ben Vorlich and the Luss hills, has played such a large part in my life that it deserves a chapter to itself.

A beautiful view of Ross Priory and Loch Lomond (courtesy of the University of Strathclyde).

The house, with its extensive grounds and gardens, was acquired by the University of Strathclyde in 1971, due to the prompt action of Sir Samuel Curran and Louis McGougan, the Bursar. A replacement for Dalandhui, the staff facility at Garelochhead, had been sought for some time and this seemed to be the answer.

Ross Priory dates back to around 1693 and is largely the work of James Gillespie (1776 - 1855), the architect known as Gillespie Graham, whose work also included St Andrew's Cathedral in Glasgow. Ross Priory was for many years owned by the Buchanan family and it was during the time of Hector Macdonald Buchanan that his friend and fellow clerk to the Court of Session in Edinburgh, Sir Walter Scott, is known to have stayed at the house. He visited at least three times (in 1810, 1816 and 1817) and it is thought that he wrote parts of 'The Lady of the Lake' and *Rob Roy* during these visits. The Scott Room, called after this distinguished guest, is maybe the very room in which Sir Walter wrote his letter to George Ellis from 'The Ross on Loch Lomond'.

In December 1973, Ross Priory was opened as a Club for staff and over the years extensive refurbishment has taken place, particularly in 1991 when private facilities were added in all the bedrooms. A lot of specialised work was done on the outside of the building and later on the addition of a lift from the ground floor to the main floor was a major and very dusty undertaking. There are 173 acres of grounds with a remarkable collection of rhododendrons and azaleas, a walled garden and greenhouses and a most attractive nine-hole golf course.

I became a member of the Ross Priory Club immediately and Iain joined as an associate member. Eventually I became a member of the Ross Priory Club Committee of Management and served on it for twenty-four years. Many years later I became an honorary member of the Club.

Iain, always a great lover of boats, had had a yacht in McAllister's Yard in Dumbarton. He was keen to have a boat again and we got a Shetland cabin cruiser, which he felt would be more suitable for an ignoramus like me than a yacht would be. She had to have a name so we studied the names in Shetland and finally settled on - not Papa Stour but *Mama Stour.*

On Inchconnachan, with the rubbish we had collected on the island.

We were fortunate in getting a mooring at Ross Priory and *Mama Stour* gave us many happy hours visiting the islands and getting to know Loch Lomond in the best possible way - from the water. Most weekends I prepared a picnic for four as we usually entertained our friends on the boat. Later we exchanged the Shetland for a Mayland cabin cruiser, which we called *Mama May.* In many ways, it was more suitable for us as the cockpit was bigger.

Beside Mama May, at Inchlonaig.

In those early days, I felt that what was needed was something to make money for Ross Priory so I organised a dinner followed by music. This was on 3rd October 1986 and it was called 'A Twiddle on the Fiddle'. The violinist was a local lady (now deceased) who played in the BBC Scottish Symphony Orchestra. She made such a fuss about it all that you would have thought she had an engagement to play in Carnegie Hall instead of in the Carnegie Room at the Priory. I had fifty-two people there and the evening was a success, which encouraged me to organise some more evenings. I refused to allow myself to be put off by the violinist's temperamental ways.

As the evenings developed, it was essential to have a name for the series, so I called them 'Lochside Productions'. Someone once said that I started them to make money for myself. I was horrified at this most unkind comment, for the exact opposite is the case, as all the events there have been heavily subsidised by me. You can call this bad management - or stupidity - if you like, but I feel it has been a great privilege to have been able to give some pleasure and enjoyment to many people, as well as support to the various artistes - quite apart from supporting Ross Priory and the University of Strathclyde.

I had, of course, heard of John Cairney but had never been to any of his performances. I noticed that he and his wife, Alannah O'Sullivan, were performing at Montgreenan near Irvine, so we booked for that. I was greatly taken with the whole thing and thought how good they would be at Ross Priory, so I invited them right away. And so began a long association with many different events.

My second evening, on 21st October 1986, was given by the Cairneys and it was called 'A Taste of Theatre' with famous theatrical extracts. I presented the evening as follows:
Act One:
The action takes place in the Bar Lounge of Ross Priory at 7.30pm. Certain characters are to be seen ordering wine for dinner.

Act Two:
Dinner (the action continues in the Dining Room between
 8 and 9pm).
Scene 1   The Iceman Cometh (melon frappé)
Scene 2   A Winter's Tale (vichyssoise)
Scene 3   Sweet Bird of Youth (supreme of chicken)
Scene 4   Bitter Sweet (lemon mousse)
Scene 5   The Desert Song (coffee)
Scene 6   Exeunt omnes to the Carnegie Room

Interval of ten minutes

Act Three:

The action continues in the Carnegie Room at 9:10pm.

Curtain Call: Same place one hour later.

This evening led to a series of 'taste' evenings with other artistes:

A Taste of Close Harmony with New Day, a group of sixteen young singers, formerly of Bishopbriggs High School.

A Taste of Grand Opera with a quartet from Opera West.

A Taste of Cranachan with Cranachan, a duo of soprano and mezzo-soprano who played recorder and clarsach respectively.

A Taste of Broadway with New Day again.

A Taste of Italy with Melisma (a soprano, a reader and a pianist).

The Cairney series continued over many years (1987 - 2001) with Dorothy Parker and Friend; Blackout, in which John Cairney re-lived his boyhood years in wartime Glasgow; The Real McGonagall, which posed the question, 'What exactly is a Real McGonagall Supper?'; Dear Aunt Jane about Jane Austen; A Ghost Evening about Robert Louis Stevenson; East End to West End, the East End of Glasgow to the West End of London; and an At Home with John Cairney.

Then the Cairneys left Glasgow for New Zealand, where Alannah's relatives lived. They stayed there for several years. There was a strange coincidence one day. A friend told me she was upset at missing a review in *The Glasgow Herald* and I said I would get it for her from the office in town, as I was going to Glasgow next day. In I went and there was John Cairney, back from New Zealand, getting photographs for a book he was writing. I could not believe my eyes!

One evening, however, deserves a special mention. John Cairney told me he was coming back to Scotland, specially to celebrate the 200th Anniversary of the death of Robert Burns and could I arrange an evening for him at Ross Priory. This was the event called 'John Anderson, our Jo' on 12th January 1996. I had mentioned to John Cairney that the University of Strathclyde was celebrating at the same time the 200th Anniversary of the death of its founder, John Anderson - hence the title of the evening - so John Cairney insisted on my presenting John Anderson and he would do Burns. In spite of my vigorous protests, I could not get out of it, so I prepared my presentation, leaving gaps for John Cairney's input on Burns. I still have the script of that, and looking back after all these years, I honestly do not know how I managed it.

That very day we picked up John from Glasgow Airport and brought him to our house. He had an appalling cold and he went straight to bed in our spare bedroom. He surfaced in the late afternoon when we had a very quick rehearsal of my text and John decided on his contribution. 'It'll be all right on the night,' as they say, and strangely it was. The evening ended with a lengthy song about John Anderson, which I had composed myself. There were sixty-nine people at this most unusual evening.

A very popular performer was George McIlwham, the brilliant flautist, now sadly deceased.

When Jane and I were going to the orchestral concerts when we were in our late teens, we had a crush on George. We went home by bus from St Enoch Square and so did George.

Fooling about with George McIlwham during a NTS cruise. He was one of the artistes on board.

We always went upstairs and we would look down expectantly to see George getting off two stops before us. If he was there that made our night but, if he was not, as occasionally happened, what a disappointment it was.

George's first performance at Ross Priory in March 1990 was with Rhona Mackay (harp) and Cameron Murdoch (piano). In March 1995, George played accompanied by David Murray (piano), the evening being called 'The Romantic Flute' and then again in October 1996 with Trio Serenata in 'Melodies of Love'. David Murray was again the pianist and the soprano was Alison Donaldson, who tragically died of a brain tumour before she was sixty. There was yet another performance in October 2008 with Trio Serenata but this time with Daisy Henderson (soprano) and Adam Magee (tenor).

A mezzo-soprano I employed a lot was Jennifer Logan. I had been at one of her concerts in Edinburgh and felt that she was ideal for my evenings and so began a long association. Her special gift was compiling hilarious programmes that were so different. Jennifer reminds me a little of Joyce Grenfell. She used to have as accompanist Dr Alan Jacques, a well-known Edinburgh psychiatrist, but latterly her accompanist has been Stuart Hope, another well-known Edinburgh musician.

Jennifer's evenings make an impressive list with intriguing titles:

1991 Cherchez la Femme
1993 Toasted Susie is My Icecream
2002 Golden Wonder (my 50th Lochside Production)
2008 Itchy Feet
2011 In the Mood
2015 Learning with Laughter (my 75th Lochside Production)
For highly original entertainment these programmes could simply not be beaten.

In the west end of Glasgow there was a company that specialised in theatre in a small space. 'Home Is Where the Art Is' put on a few events for me and they made a nice change from the musical evenings. We had 'Kissing and Telling' in 1998, 'Mae West - All of Me' in 2000 and 'Love Letters' in 2002.

I was privileged to become friendly with Alison Stephens, who was the UK's top mandolin-player. She played the mandolin in the film *Captain Corelli's Mandolin* and spent three years touring the UK with the stage version. I first heard her playing in that in the Pitlochry Festival Theatre with a pianist I knew and I sought her out thereafter. I had a very happy relationship with her. She first played for me in 2004 in 'A Mandolin Journey' with Anne Evans (piano); then in 2006 with Craig Ogden (guitar) in 'A Plucky Pair'. I used to make Alison laugh by referring to Craig as dishy! Later in 2009, she played again at Ross Priory, this time with Lauren Scott (harp).

Alison made her professional debut at the age of seventeen in the Barbican in London. She was the first graduate in mandolin from Trinity College of Music in London and became Professor of Mandolin there immediately. It was a terrible heartbreak when she developed cervical cancer in 2008 and died at the age of forty in October 2010.

In 1991 Anne Lorne Gillies performed as Lady Nairne. John Kenny, a brilliant trombonist, played the alphorn in 1992. A friend in the audience became famous as the chap who supported the bell of the alphorn on his shoulder while John Kenny played it! On a return visit in 2010 he played the Celtic war horn known as the carnyx. The Dunedin Consort gave us a recital of 'Vocal Pyrotechnics' in 2004 and we had two memorable and hilarious evenings 'Travelling by Tuba' in 1999 and in 2005.

Those were just a few of the unusual evenings I had at Ross Priory. There was always an audience of between fifty and sixty and I put into the University coffers over £67,000 for the food served on these occasions. I have no idea what money was spent on drinks as guests bought their own. The Lochside Productions will continue when the nights are light as this avoids driving in the dark.

In 2015 I started a new series of entertainments - afternoon tea with professional musicians. I call them the 'Tahiti Trots' after

Ross Priory with the hills above Luss just visible in the distance (courtesy of the University of Strathclyde).

Shostakovich's orchestration of Tea for Two from No, No, Nanette by Vincent Youmans. These events are very relaxed and informal. They are held only on Monday, Tuesday, Wednesday or Thursday during the spring and summer months and at random intervals. They are proving very popular. I composed the following suitable words for the song which is like a sort of signature tune, played at the beginning of each event.

Tea for two,
For me, for you
And many more,
Perhaps three score,
And music too,
Arranged for your delight.

To answer your queries -
It's Katharine's smart series
To give lots of pleasure
And enrich your leisure,
Showcasing the talents
Of splendid musicians too...so...

We'd recommend
You bring a friend
To share with you
The lovely view
And to enjoy the grounds
And gardens too.

Come and join the Tahiti Trot
At this delightful
Lochside spot.
You'll love a lot
The Priory's special tea.

I think that probably sums things up quite nicely.

18 - Retirement on the Horizon

'Twice as much husband and half as much money' (anon)

That is evidently someone's slightly jaundiced idea of retirement but definitely not mine. It reminds me a little of the woman who said she'd married her husband for better or for worse but not for lunch! As far as I was concerned 'twice as much husband' suited me fine.

When I was about fifty-one I received a letter from the University offering me retirement under the Government's Premature Retirement Compensation Scheme. I was quite shocked - no thanks - I did not want to retire. However, two years later, the letter was repeated. By that time I had discovered that several members of staff had opted for it and so I decided to have the financial situation examined and the result was too good to turn down. I therefore planned to retire at the end of September 1984 and take the part-time option, which lasted for three years. As it is not possible to produce publications part-time, my suggestion was that I should work for the first terms of the next three sessions, during which time I would produce certain publications. I think I had to work for seventy-one days - it was a strange number - but I always stayed on to complete the work in hand. My suggestion met with approval and it resulted in my 'retiring' on a Friday and coming back after the weekend to start my part-time option on the Monday. It was a strange situation but it worked quite well. For the rest of the session I was off completely. During this time I kept up all my usual activities.

We had been in our villa in Waterfoot for about ten years and in 1980 I was beginning to think that it was no longer necessary for us to have two double bedrooms and a single bedroom and that we should move with an eye on retirement. Iain agreed with me and so we started our search for a suitable house. As we were both still working, our time for house-hunting was limited. We used to go away in the car on a Saturday with a picnic and *The Glasgow Herald* property supplement. We wished to move to the Loch Lomond area so that we could enjoy the boat. Although the boat was kept in a barbed-wire enclosure it got vandalised more than once and we were getting decidedly fed up with it. Of course, finding a suitable property was easier said than done. We saw lots of nice houses over a very wide area, but none that was ideal. Very often we found that there was too much land involved, such as paddocks and so on, and we did not wish that. Believe it or not, this went on for eighteen months without success.

One day I said to Iain, 'Let's draw up a list of the things we really want,' as the lack of progress was beginning to get us down. This was our list, but not in any order of priority:

1.   a house all on the one level
2.   a separate dining-room and kitchen (ie not open plan)
3.   a flat, easily managed garden
4.   room to keep the boat beside us
5.   the ability to stop our cars at our property (this was by no means the case at some of the properties we saw)
6.   a nice outlook
7.   reasonably private, but not isolated

A tall order, you might say, and you would be right. By this time it was early in 1982 and, shortly after drawing up our list, I saw an advert in *The Glasgow Herald*, which said:

For Sale - three-year-old house in Gartocharn.

A view of the village of Gartocharn with Duncryne, taken from the road to Ross Priory.

We went to see it right away and once was enough. We bought it immediately from a gentleman who lived outside the village. It had been built for his mother, a Mrs Walker, whom he brought over from Edinburgh to be nearer him, when she was widowed.

The house was all on the one level, except that there was a proper stair up to a forty-nine-foot loft, which could have been converted into bedrooms or whatever, but that was something we did not want to do. There was a large lounge, a separate dining-room, a large master bedroom with ensuite facilities, a large kitchen and bathroom, and a spare bedroom, large enough for two beds. There was a lot of mostly flat ground round the house, and lots of room for the boat and our cars. The house looked towards Loch Lomond and was behind a house on the main road, and up an un-named private road, secluded but by no means isolated. We could walk to the village shop, the hall, Gartocharn Church, and the school, and Ross Priory was about one and a half miles away.

Of course, after thirty-four years, much has been done to the house and the ground has been developed into a garden. It was ideal for us. We could hardly believe our luck. We moved in August 1982 and we commuted to Glasgow for four years. We got up at 6.30am, left at 7.30am and were in town before 8.30am. We thought nothing of it. As there are many Mrs Walkers in the world, it was some time before we discovered that the Mrs Walker, who had lived in our new house for three years, was none other than Alison Blackie, the sister of Walter Graham Blackie, who was the Chairman when I was an editor in Blackie's in the 1950s. It was their father who had commissioned the Hill House in Helensburgh from Charles Rennie Mackintosh and they had been brought up there. So I felt that our new home had been meant for me. What a strange coincidence!

We had not been long in Gartocharn when we discovered that the local Burns Club- the Kilmaronock Burns Club - was looking for a Secretary and Treasurer. So we took on these jobs. Iain was Treasurer for many years and I was Secretary for twenty-three years, during which time I organised forty-six functions - a St Andrew's Night and a Burns Supper each year. We also gave an annual entertainment at Erskine, taking with us lots of home-baking, until one night they asked us to discontinue this event as they had too many. Latterly I felt I was going to outlive the Burns Club and I did. Very sadly, in 2008 it closed down, due to lack of support. It was suggested to me that I should organise a Burns Supper myself, so I have had one annually since then at Ross Priory.

Iain was always very interested in the management of money - and was very good at it, too. In 1987 he set up an Investment Club in the village. I acted as Club Secretary for three years to help him get it established. It was highly successful and is still going strong.

It is at this point that I would now like to mention the Order of St John, which played a big part in Iain's life and still does in mine. In 1888 Queen Victoria made the Order a Royal Order of Chivalry with the monarch as its Sovereign Head. Since then the Grand Prior has always been a member of the Royal Family. At present it is His Royal Highness the Duke of Gloucester. The Scottish Priory was formed in 1947.

It all started with us when a friend of Iain's urged us to join the Glasgow St John Association, which we did. In those days, the 'Associations' were the fund-raising arms of the Order and anyone interested could join. Nowadays, there are no Associations and such members are called Priory Members, involved in similar fund-raising and other activities. There are twelve Area Committees in Scotland, which raise funds for local charitable projects and to support St John's work at home and overseas, particularly the Eye Hospital in Jerusalem.

It must be stressed that Priory Members are not members of the Order of St John as this is an honour conferred by Her Majesty the Queen as the Sovereign Head of the Order. You have to be proposed, approved, and admitted to the Order. In 1984 I was admitted, I became an Officer in 1990 and Commander in 2008. Iain was admitted in 1991 and became an Officer in 1995. We were both devoted to the Order, and I still am. There is an Annual Festival, held in different Scottish cities or towns on or around 24th June, St John's Day. This takes the form of a church service

Outside St Cuthbert's Church, Edinburgh, after being admitted to the Order of St John, 1984.

with Communion, followed by an Investiture and a lunch. There is usually a Civic Reception on the previous evening.

For some time, I was the Secretary of a new committee - the St John Music Committee. The idea was to put on an annual concert, in different venues, in aid of St John. Unfortunately, this was not very successful for various reasons and the committee was disbanded. The Chairman was June Gordon, the Marchioness of Aberdeen. When the St John Festival was in Aberdeen, she invited Iain and me to tea, so off we went to Haddo House. We were admitted at a side door and ushered into the huge drawing-room. The massive grand piano was covered with photographs, many of them of the Royal Family. Lady Aberdeen brought in the tea tray herself. I remember thinking that the rock buns were appropriately named. At one point in the proceedings a young man entered, after knocking, and whispered something very confidential to our hostess. When he left, she turned to us and said, 'My personal standard is wrapping itself round the flagpole'. When we departed, I said to Iain, 'Well, that 's a problem we won't ever have'.

Another Society we became members of was the St Andrew Society of Glasgow. (You must say 'of Glasgow' because the Edinburgh Society regards itself as *the* St Andrew Society!) The Honorary President then was the Earl of Mansfield. We attended meetings, talks, dinners and outings regularly and then one day I was asked to go on the Council. The Chairman was a lecturer in German at the University of Strathclyde and I knew him slightly. After some time he surprised me by telling me that he wished to resign as Chairman and wanted me to take over. I was absolutely amazed as I had no intention of doing any such thing, but he was adamant about it. So I found myself Chairman of the Council for three years. I was not too popular as I can think of two people who wanted the job but there was nothing I could do about it. The position involved a great deal of hard work, as there were many things to arrange. The President was Sir Robin McLellan, a most charming person, whom I liked enormously. The unfortunate thing was that he was diagnosed with cancer and died in June 1991 which saddened us all greatly, and I found myself having to carry out the President's duties as well as my own. I chaired two dinners in the Banqueting Hall of the City Chambers in Glasgow. At the dinner in November 1991, the distinguished line-up of speakers included Jack Webster, the well-known journalist, who proposed the Toast to Scotland Yet. Emeritus Professor Tom Carbery, who had been a Senior Professor in the Strathclyde

Business School and who was a great friend of mine for many years, proposed the Toast to the City of Glasgow. The reply to the Toast was given by Morrison Dunbar, a well-known business man, whose hobby was music. He was a very fine violinist and led the Glasgow Chamber Orchestra. I played the oboe with his string quartet on certain occasions. In 1987 he became Chairman of the Board of Governors of the Royal Scottish Academy of Music and Drama and in 1991 he was Lord Dean of Guild of the Merchants' House. He is still much to the fore at concerts in Glasgow. The Toast to the Scot Abroad was proposed by James Mackay, who had been the editor of the *Burns Chronicle* and whose volumes on Burns I regard as unsurpassed.

I remember I tried to get Rikki Fulton to propose the Toast to the City of Glasgow. I had heard him give a magnificent epilogue at the Hogmanay event on TV and I was much impressed and felt it would be marvellous at our next dinner. However, he did not accept my invitation, which was a blow! I still have his letter. Here is a part of what he said:

Thank you for your kind letter and your flattering invitation to speak at your next annual dinner, but I am afraid I have to disappoint you.
While I am delighted that you thought so highly of the 'Epilogue', it serves to make the point that the agony I suffered in its creation, and which I used to suffer in the preparation of speeches generally has, for many, many years now, made me follow my rule never to undertake speaking engagements.'

Well, who would have thought it?

It was the Chairman of the Council's job to organise the annual day out for the Society. This was more difficult than you would imagine. The pattern of the event was always departure in the coach from Park Road at 9.30am, followed by coffee somewhere at 11am. To keep the cost down many of us had a packed lunch, but it was essential to have shelter of some sort arranged for eating our lunch in case of inclement weather. There had also to be the opportunity available to purchase lunch for those who wished to do so. Then there was a high tea around 5.30pm. It could be difficult to find a hotel which was willing to provide such a thing. Of course, there was also the timing to consider because we had to be at the various stops at the right time. So Iain and I always tried out the outings in our car, so that I knew exactly what the arrangements were on the day. There was the all-important choice of the tour, which had to be manageable. It was all quite tricky.

The University held a retiral event at which all male staff were presented with University ties and female staff with scarves, which I have never seen anyone wearing. The spouses of those retiring were each given a University diary. When it came to our turn, Graham Hills could not find Iain to give him his diary. When he did see him, he said, 'Oh, there you are, Iain. I did not know you with your trousers on!' Of course, I understood the reason for this odd remark which was that the Principal had been used to seeing Iain at the University functions with his kilt on. What other people made of it, I hate to think! Towards the end of September 1984 my own retirement took place. Iain himself was fortunate, too, in getting early retirement in July 1986. I had still one more term to work and I came off the books, as they say, in September 1987.

When we were both completely free of our jobs, I thought how nice it would be to go back to dancing lessons. Then I dismissed the idea completely from my mind saying to myself, 'We'll be arguing about steps all the time. Forget it!' Well, it was like telepathy. Shortly after this Iain said to me - completely out of the blue - that he had arranged for us to have private ballroom and Latin American lessons with Warren Brown, who was a Scottish Dance Champion, and we were to go to the Masonic Hall in Dumbarton at 5.30pm on a certain date. This began an association of many years with Warren, which I enjoyed enormously. We had lessons in many different places. The official practice time for the Dancing School was held in a hall on a Friday night, so we went to that. Over the years we developed huge, long routines for all ten dances, which were:

Ballroom - Viennese Waltz, modern waltz, quickstep, slow foxtrot and tango - and
Latin American - cha-cha, rumba, samba, paso doble and jive.

I loved the challenge of getting new steps, mastering them, and then getting them fitted into our routines.

Naturally we became friendly with other dancers and we were founder members of a Tea Dance Club which met weekly. I do not think that a single one of us thought that the Tea Dance Club would last long but it lasted for thirteen and a half years. We met at 2pm, danced for an hour, had a half-hour tea-break, and danced till 4.30pm. We kept to our partners and so had a good opportunity to practise our steps but there were many novelty dances on offer as well. This meant that, at that time, we were dancing three times a week.

We also went to the Dance Championships which took the form of a dinner with the various competitions interspersed through the general dancing. One night I was sitting beside a former Scottish Champion. He made the remark to me - with some feeling, I may say - that when it came to dancing Scottish men were a dead loss. It was the women who kept it all going. That I could well believe.

At the Dance Championships

At another Championship the Chairman made an announcement, which told us we were all to put our hands under our seats. So I felt under my seat and found an envelope, which contained a voucher for £150 towards a professional photographic portrait.

We thought that this was too much to ignore so we investigated the situation.

The voucher was from a photographer in Innerleithen, beyond Peebles. We made an appointment with him and he told us to bring two sets of clothes for the photographic session. Everything about it was arranged by him - the clothes we wore, the way we were positioned, where our hands were, and so on. He told us that what we were doing was something lots of couples wished they had done, but most never got round to it. It was quite a lengthy business. I was not aware of any background to the photographs but, of course, all that had been carefully considered too.

We had arranged to spend the night at a local hotel. In the normal way of things, clients had to return at a later date to view the photographs but, when the photographer realised how far away we lived, he said he would have the photographs ready to view the next day, which was most obliging of him.

At the viewing session two photographs were displayed side by side on a screen and we had to accept one and reject the other. This went on until we had our final choice of a large framed photograph of us both and a folder consisting of a central, different photograph of us both, with a photograph of Iain alone on one side and of me alone on the other. We were then ready to place our order and pay accordingly.

It all cost a great deal more than £150 but we were told quite clearly that the voucher was only a contribution towards the final cost. We had to pay a return visit later on to collect the finished articles. It had all been quite an experience and one we would never regret because they were such lovely things to have. We thought ourselves very lucky.

The folder of photographs we chose after the session with the photographer at Innerleithen.

There was one thing I considered very important in my marriage and that was that Iain should have every opportunity to pursue his special interests. As well as boats, he loved cars and aeroplanes. He celebrated his retirement by arranging a flight for us in a small plane from Glasgow Airport. We had to stand by, as it were, until the weather conditions were just right and await a summons from the airport. We did not have to wait too long and we got word to report at an office at the airport, where we were treated like VIPs. The plane was tiny. Iain was in the front looking like Biggles. A young pilot was at the controls and I was behind Iain feeling terrified out of my wits and praying that the pilot would not have a heart attack. The idea was to fly over our house, which we did, and then up Loch Lomond and over to Loch Katrine. We were asked whether we wished to go back the same way or over the city and we chose to come back over Glasgow. The visibility was superb and it was all a memorable experience. Whenever possible we went to airshows. I loved them and it was always a special treat to see the Red Arrows. Iain would have liked to join the RAF but his eyesight was not good enough. Nevertheless he enjoyed his time with the Royal Engineers in Kuala Lumpur.

Iain's great ambition was to own a vintage car and eventually he got a 1964 Daimler, which was his pride and joy, as well as his big red Volvo. By this time we had a block of three garages built - there was loads of room for them. The boat was in the largest one and the other two housed the Volvo and the Daimler. (You can guess whose car sat outside, can't you?) We joined the Scottish Western Thoroughbred Vehicle Club and went to meetings and rallies - a very new experience for me. *The Glasgow Herald* wanted to have an article about the Daimler, so one snowy day a reporter called to interview Iain about it. With the snow on the ground the car could not be taken out very easily, but a photograph of Iain was taken beside the car in the garage. It was published beside the article, which was entitled 'There's Nothing Like a Daimler'.

Iain's Volvo which we loved and which served us so well. When I came to sell it, I felt as if I were betraying an old friend.

Iain with his 1964 Daimler, his pride and joy.

One day I got a telephone call asking me to be Vice-President of the Park School Seniors' Association. As I had never kept up with the school, this was a very big surprise indeed. The President wanted me as her Vice -President and I agreed to take on the job. This was in 1994, and in 1995 I became President, which involved me in a great deal of work - arranging meetings, sending out letters to the members and chairing the annual dinner in the Royal Scottish Automobile Club, a most delightful venue. I will not easily forget the day near the end of my term of office when the Chairman of the School Governors telephoned me to tell me that Park was amalgamating with Laurel Bank. What a shock! It was not a success and soon Park School was no more. I was very sad about the demise of my school but it seemed that nothing could save it. In those days, girls' schools were joining up with boys' schools.

We were very fortunate in that we did a lot of travelling over many years during our retirement. So now it's time for a new chapter.

19 - Travel for Travel's Sake

And all pre-terrorism

I have often heard it said that there is nothing as boring as other people's holidays. As travelling took up a fair bit of our retirement I hope I may be forgiven for mentioning some of our experiences in our efforts to see the world.

We were very fond of America and visited it on several occasions. Our first visit was in 1980 when we took The Golden West Adventure Tour by coach from Los Angeles, visiting several places en route to San Francisco and Sacramento. We then went over the Sierra Nevada, going through the Donner Pass, famous because of the family who got trapped in the snow and began to eat each other. Reno, Virginia City, Ponderosa Ranch at Lake Tahoe, and Carson City, the capital of Nevada, were all in the tour. Next was Yosemite Park (in California again), which must surely be one of the most beautiful places in the world, and then we left for Las Vegas via the four-hundred-mile-long Nevada desert. The Grand Canyon in Arizona was a fantastic sight and in Scottsdale it was so hot we could only stay by the hotel pool. When we got back to California we spent the night at Palm Springs and went to Disneyland the next day. When we returned to Los Angeles we went to a different hotel - somewhat unexpectedly. I knew that at this time the Scottish National Orchestra Chorus was to be in the States but I did not know the details of their trip. I knew one or two people in the Chorus, particularly Dr Clifford Bartlett, who was in the Mathematics Department in the University of Strathclyde. When we stepped out of the lift on our way to dinner there was Cliff in the lobby - of all the people in America! What a strange coincidence!

Iain was very keen to explore New York State by car. We did that for four weeks in September - October 1987. This was a fabulous and very unusual holiday. After four days in New York City with a room on the twentieth floor in the Hotel Lexington, we picked up our car - a Ford Tempo - so I called this holiday 'Touring in Tempo'. It took a lot of courage to drive in New York City but eventually we got away from the congestion and went up the Hudson Valley to West Point at the US Military Academy which was in a vast parkland. A wooded path had a notice which said:

FLIRTATION WALK.
NO ENTRY UNLESS ACCOMPANIED BY A CADET.

In the museum there - the only building we were able to go into - we saw, amongst other exhibits, a capsule of the type used for the atomic bomb and Einstein's letter to Roosevelt, warning him of its likely development and urging him to be extremely vigilant. We next went to a small town called Poughkeepsie (P'kipsie) and found that it was celebrating its 300th Anniversary with a buffet meal for 450 people in the hotel where we spent the night. We had come to see Hyde Park, the Roosevelts' house, which was a simply furnished family home. Further up the road was the Vanderbilt Mansion, in beautiful parkland sweeping down to the Hudson, a huge elaborate mansion left to the nation by the Vanderbilts, who had no heirs. We then went west to Cooperstown, which has retained the serenity of the village founded in 1786 by the father of James Fenimore Cooper, author of *The Last of the Mohicans*. Fenimore House, the HQ of the New York State Historical Association, and owned by the nation, was a beautiful mansion with period furniture and American art. The chief guide here had been a headmaster in Yorkshire!

Our next stop was Owego, where we got fixed up for the night very happily in Thompson Park House on the main street but backing on to the Susquehanna River. This was a most elegant house, 120 years old, with several guest rooms, all beautifully furnished. The lady of the house was Honesty Buczek, whose Polish husband was away on business. Nevertheless, she had plenty of company - a huge Rhodesian Ridgeback called Bogart; an Australian Shepherd puppy called Katie; a calico cat called Cally; a canary called Mozart; and two budgies with Polish names. Owego was in Indian country which was obvious from the place names. We were told that, when the white man came, the Indians said, 'O, we go!'

We left next morning for Corning to go to the Glass Centre, where there were three areas to visit - the Museum of Glass, the Hall of Science and Industry, and the Steuben Glass Factory. The special exhibition on at the time was 'Glass of the Caesars', the greatest exhibition of Roman glass ever assembled. We left Corning for Watkin's Glen on Lake Seneca in the Finger Lakes. Although many places in this area have names of classical origin, Lake Seneca, the River Seneca and the Seneca Falls are all named after the Seneca Indians and not after the Roman statesman and philosopher.

Next day the weather was so bad that we decided to go straight to the Niagara Falls, where we got into the Holiday Inn for one night only. Suitably clad for the wet weather, we explored the Falls on the American side and walked over Rainbow Bridge for a better view from the Canadian side. We went aboard *The Maid of the Mist* to see the Horseshoe Falls. It was a great experience to get so close to the thundering water and to be enveloped in the mist and spray.

After enjoying a fantastic view from the observation floor of the Skylon Tower, we returned to the USA!

Another wet day, so we didn't 'shuffle off to Buffalo', but went to the Aquarium, Whirlpool State Park and Power Vista, the free visitor centre of the New York Power Company. We found the American exhibitions wonderful and this one showed how they harnessed the river to provide thirty-eight per cent of New York State's electricity.

We left Niagara Falls and reached the shores of Lake Ontario en route to Rochester, but first Iain wanted to see Lockport on the Erie Canal, where there was a lock where the water rose 180 feet in three steps. Three boats were going through; one of them was the *Wayzgoose* which interested me particularly as very few people know what a wayzgoose is. It is an annual dinner of employees in the printing trade.

Rochester, on the Genesee River, is the third largest city in New York State. There the International Museum of Photography is housed in the George Eastman House. George Eastman (1854 - 1932) founded in 1880 the Eastman Kodak Company. His inventive genius made photography available to millions of people. We then headed south-east to Canandaigua, back in the Finger Lakes. We had a memorable visit to the Sonnenberg Mansion and Gardens. The owner, Frederick Thompson, and a partner, George Baker, founded the First National City Bank of New York. Frederick died in 1899 and his wife, Mary, created the nine magnificent gardens between 1902 and 1916 as a memorial to her husband.

We next wanted to head in the direction of the Adirondacks and after Erie Canal Village, we stopped at Saranac Lake, where there is a Robert Louis Stevenson Memorial Cottage at 11 Stevenson Lane, where RLS lived from 1887-88 while undergoing treatment for tuberculosis. The cottage was closed that day. We left for Lake Placid about ten miles away, digressing to see the spectacular Olympic Ski Jumps, where an elevator takes you up twenty-six storeys to the top of the ninety-metre ski jump. Lake Placid had been host to the Winter Olympic Games in 1932 and also in 1980. Although the Lake was pretty, we agreed that it was nothing like as beautiful as Loch Lomond.

Next day we crossed Lake Champlain to Burlington in Vermont and the following day we went to the Shelburne Museum, set in forty-five acres of park with many buildings housing various collections. The 220-foot steam paddlewheeler, the *SS Ticonderoga*, hauled over two miles of land from Lake Champlain, is 'docked' there. After a visit to the capital of Vermont, Montpelier, with its magnificent Capitol building, we headed east to the coast of Maine which is 3,000 miles long as there are so many inlets and peninsulas. We spent the weekend at Boothbay Harbour, a busy and expensive area. We felt that the New Englanders lived off chowder and lobster. We then went south towards Portland, driving through dull scenery. There we visited a house where John Paul Jones had been a lodger. He was the Scot from Kirkcudbrightshire who became the father of the American Navy.

Well, we made it to Boston and gave up the car, having driven about 2,000 miles. I loved Boston and it was such a thrill to walk round the campuses of Harvard University and Massachusetts Institute of Technology across the Charles River. So ended a holiday full of memories to last a lifetime.

We went back to the States, several times, going right across Alaska, enjoying jazz in New Orleans and going up and down a bit of the Mississippi, and exploring Florida.

Enjoying jazz in New Orleans

A streetcar in New Orleans, but not named 'Desire'.

The City of the Dead. In New Orleans there is so little earth that bodies cannot be buried.

All aboard for the Mississippi!

Iain wanted to tour British Columbia by car and we did that in 1981. We just loved it. After three glorious days in Vancouver we got our car. It was a beauty - a deep cream Ford Fairmont, automatic, air-conditioned, and with power-assisted steering. We had been asked to visit a lady in Victoria called Mollie Boyd and we thought that for fun we would call the car after her but when we saw that the registration number was JJP 007 it just had to be Mollie Bond! The scenery everywhere in the Rockies was breath-taking. We went to Banff and went up Sulphur Mountain in the cable car. We stayed in the Chateau on Lake Louise and walked to the far end of Lake Victoria. Next day we left for the Columbia Icefields and went on a snowmobile down the steepest, unpaved public road in North America.

We reached Jasper in the late afternoon. We had been told that this was the only place we would need to book in advance but, although we tried to do so, we were not successful. Nevertheless, we arrived there, ever hopeful. Iain stopped beside a hotel on the main road and I went in to try to book a room but no joy. The lady in Reception said to her husband, who happened to be standing nearby, 'Take this lady round to the house, Ben'. When we got there he handed us the keys of the house after he had shown us our room. Wasn't that amazing? I do not think I would have done that to complete strangers. We enjoyed it so much that we stayed for two nights. On leaving Jasper we were able to see Mount Robson (12,974 feet) the highest peak in the Rockies - a truly magnificent sight.

We went to Vancouver Island and visited the amazing Butchart Gardens. One night we went to a Lebanese restaurant which displayed a notice saying:

'A Belly Dancer performs here at lunch time.'

Ah well, we thought, we'll miss that, thank goodness! However, there were twelve people celebrating something at a long table and suddenly the bead curtain rattled and out came the belly dancer! She did her best to wobble about and, although pretty, she did not have enough of what it takes, nor was she swarthy enough!

It was on this holiday that I developed a passion for oysters - not raw - but cooked in different ways. Oysters Rockefeller were superb. Before our flight home I particularly wanted to see Simon Fraser University and the University of British Columbia. On our return to Scotland someone asked me if I was back in God's own country. 'No,' I replied, 'I've just come from it'. On another holiday we went to Toronto, Ottawa, Montreal, Nova Scotia and Newfoundland. But British Columbia remained our favourite.

We did not see a lot of South America, but we did take a cruise from Fort Lauderdale in Florida, calling at St Thomas, Guadaloupe, Bridgetown in Barbados, Devil's Island, Belem, Santerem, Alter do Chao, Boca do Valerio - up the Amazon to Manaus, in the middle of the Brazilian Rain Forest, from where we flew to Miami en route for home. On another occasion we went through the Panama Canal, calling first at Caracas in Venezuela and Cartagena in Colombia, where we saw the fabulous emeralds, and later visiting Costa Rica, which we liked enormously.

We explored Europe for many years, sometimes by going on rivers, which we found to be a great way to see a country. After some time in Prague we went on the Elbe from Litomerice in the Czech Republic to Wittenberg, where we disembarked and went to Potsdam and Berlin. We spent Christmas one year, going on the Danube from Passau to Budapest and back, calling at Melk, Vienna and Bratislava. The Dutch waterways from Amsterdam to Antwerp were fascinating. It was sometimes difficult to tell whether the water was the sea, a river or a canal. What a marvellous river the Rhine is! We much enjoyed our holiday on it from Cologne to Basel with many stops in between and taking in also a bit of the Mosel. However the Rhone from Avignon to Lyon presented us with problems due to flooding and bad weather. We had been in the Algarve and in Lisbon and Estoril in Portugal but what was even more interesting was going up the Douro from Oporto to the Spanish border, and back down.

At the border between Portugal and Spain, after a trip up the Douro from Oporto.

We had a Christmas in Helsinki one year which was memorable and it was so nice to see it again one July when we were on a cruise to the Balkan capitals. We did the Norwegian coastal voyage right up to the Russian border and down again to Bergen in the Coastal Express. We went on a Russian ship right through the Mediterranean and the Black Sea to Odessa and then flew to Moscow for a few days. We had a double cruise to the Far East in 1989, starting with three days in Bangkok and joining the *Pacific Princess* at Sattahip, from where we cruised to Singapore, Bali, Kota Kinabalu in Borneo, Manila, Hong Kong, Shanghai, Pusan in South Korea, Nagasaki in Japan and Dalian and Beijing in China. We were in Tiananmen Square three weeks before the troubles began, and we realised afterwards that we had witnessed the start of them.

As the result of an unexpected leaflet in the mail, we had an amazing holiday in February 1994 in Zimbabwe and Zambia which enabled us to see the Victoria Falls in both countries and many other sights. We also had a day-trip to Botswana. Truly the Victoria Falls must be one of the most wonderful sights in the world.

We were particularly fond of Switzerland and visited many areas there as well as Austria and Italy. We went round the Pyrenees (up France and down Spain) and later went to Andalucia and Gibraltar. We much enjoyed Yugoslavia (when it still was one country). Lake Bled and Dubrovnik were delightful and contrasting places to visit. Before I got married I had been to Greece, but as Iain was so keen on boats and sailing we had a holiday on a catamaran going round the Ionian Islands and one on Elba with yachts, both of which were a bit hair-raising for me!

In 2000 we went to the Passion Play at Oberammergau. It began at 9.30am. Lunch was 12 noon till 3pm when the play continued till 6.20pm. It was so realistic that you felt you were actually there. It is a tremendous undertaking for the locals, who go back to their jobs when not performing. Everything was so expensive that all I could afford was a tiny wee carved rabbit. It is lovely and I am glad I have it as a memento of a wonderful experience.

We never got to South Africa, Australia or New Zealand but I think we did rather well. So that was our 'Travel, for Travel's Sake', like Robert Louis Stevenson, but we didn't have a donkey!

20 - Charities Galore

'It is more blessed to give than to receive' (Acts 20. 35)

By 1997 Iain had set up his Charitable Trust, which was called The John Liston Scottish Charitable Trust. It had to be called that, because Iain had been christened John after his father, but he was never called John. If I had had anything to do with it I would have called it the John (Iain) Liston Scottish Charitable Trust, but I knew little about it at that time. Although there were three other Trustees besides the two of us, Iain dealt with the Trust himself. Occasionally he might ask for my opinion about something, but I was seldom involved. The donations were all £100 or multiples of £100 and this went on for several years.

It was round about this time that I began to feel that Iain was becoming very vague about things and it was the start of many difficult years, as he became worse and was finally diagnosed as having progressive supranuclear palsy, a rare particularly dreadful illness, which - you may recall - Dudley Moore died of. For a while he had to go three times a week to the Joint Hospital in Dumbarton for assessment. I hated leaving him there. Even now, when I pass the Joint Hospital, it gives me the creeps. He very much enjoyed being in the car and for two years I drove 36,000 miles taking him out in his big red Volvo. When I could no longer cope, I managed to get him into a Nursing Home in Callander, which I visited regularly for two years until he died in June 2007. What a heartbreak it all was. I continued to visit the Nursing Home every week for the next three years, as by then I had got friendly with one of the residents who loved Scrabble and I became her Scrabble partner until she died.

It was then that it became essential for me to deal with the Charitable Trust. I soon realised that it was a great deal of constant work, as the appeals for funding kept coming in. It began to occupy a lot of my life. As I came to the conclusion that donations of £100, or multiples of £100, were rather a waste of time and effort, I adopted the policy of having donations of £1,000 and multiples of £1,000.

I soon became very aware of the different kinds of letters that came in. There were those that were so bossy, suggesting that the Trust should give them £10,000; those that enclosed masses and masses of reports, financial statements and other literature, which were of no interest to me and were decidedly off-putting; and there were those with such a nice, modest tone about them that won me over so easily. The sheer number of charities never ceases to amaze me.

I always felt that the Trust money was Iain's and not mine, although the Stockbroker said it was mine. Nevertheless I continued to feel that I was looking after Iain's money and I kept in mind charities that would have interested him. I appointed my Tax Adviser as the Trust Manager and he and the Stockbroker did a great job and were such a support to me.

I hope that this chapter does not give the impression of boasting. I would like to emphasise that boasting does not come into it. The fact of the matter was that the money was there for distribution - it was my job to distribute it and that is what I did.

Although it was hard work, there was much of interest as well and so I would like to share with you some of my experiences in dealing with the Trust. Most of the charities mentioned here were supported annually for several years. I have tried to group them under suitable headings.

Hospitals, Hospices and Homes

As Iain had been in the Royal Engineers, he was keen to support Erskine, that marvellous place for ex-servicemen and women near the east side of the Erskine Bridge. St Andrew's Hospice (Airdrie), St Vincent's Hospice (Howwood), the Highland Hospice (Inverness) and Harlington Hospice (Bedfordshire) were all supported. I also gave money to Leuchie House in North Berwick, which provides respite short breaks with twenty-four-hour nursing care. For some time the Trust had been supporting the Little Sisters of the Poor through their St Joseph's Residential Home in Robroyston in the north of Glasgow, and this became very appropriate when my dear friend, the Very Rev James Canon Simcox retired there from St Martin's in Renton. His Diamond Jubilee in the priesthood was splendidly celebrated in St Joseph's on 21st June 2013 and it was a great privilege to be there. After a service in the chapel, attended by many other priests and conducted by the Archbishop of Glasgow, Philip Tartaglia, there was a delightful meal in a large hall. To my utter astonishment I was seated at the Archbishop's right side, Jim being on his left side. I thought this was a mistake, as I had expected to be seated beside the friends who had come with me, but I was assured that it was not a mistake. I liked the Archbishop very much indeed and I was able to ask him about the Tartaglia who had played the horn in the Glasgow Orchestral Society when I was in it, and he told me that was his uncle who was now ninety. However, most of the talking was done by Jim!

Charities dealing with diseases

There are, of course, many cancer charities and it was impossible to support them all. Cancer Support Scotland (Tak Tent), Professor Kenneth Calman's charity, which describes itself as 'one to one support for cancer patients', was always on our list, as was Marie Curie Cancer Care. Action Medical Research (for children), the Peach Unit (Paediatric Epidemiology and Community Health) and Asthma Relief were also among the beneficiaries. Since our policy was to support things Scottish, Tenovus Scotland (medical research) was a firm favourite. I often thought that Research was the Cinderella of the charities. Many years ago I was invited along with other supporters, to afternoon tea with our then patron, HRH Princess Margaret, in the Western Infirmary, Glasgow. I did not think she was well and shortly after that she had a lung operation. Much more recently, we had a visit from our present patron, HRH The Princess Royal, in the Royal College of Physicians and Surgeons, Glasgow. She took a great interest in the presentations of research given by some of those who had benefited from grants from Tenovus Scotland and then spent time with the supporters who were standing in groups round a large hall. She shook everyone's hand and asked my group why we supported this charity. I replied, 'Because it is nice to support something that is particularly Scottish and medical research deserves support'. I also gave money to the Muscular Dystrophy Campaign and to the Spina Bifida Association.

Charities that support people with disabilities

I feel very sympathetic towards Scottish Autism, as autism is such a strange abnormality. I knew someone whose autistic son said one word, 'mummy,' and nothing else ever, and who lived in an institution all his life. His father, now dead, visited him faithfully. As far as I know, this person is still alive. What a heartbreak! A brilliant organist, who sometimes plays at the Scottish Cinema Organ Trust's concerts, has two autistic sons, now grown up, but unable to look after themselves. He himself set up a charity some time ago to support autistic people. He told me that he and his wife worried about who would look after the boys, if anything happened to them. I also know devoted parents, who have an autistic son and a normal son. It is a very strange condition and, as far as I am aware, little is known about it, so anything that can support or bring relief is worthwhile.

The Royal National Institute for the Blind and the Royal Blind Society also received regular donations. When I first received an appeal from the Eyeless Trust, which supported people born without eyes, I felt very upset indeed. Now the Eyeless Trust has merged with the Royal Blind Society. Deafness is another severe and very isolating disability so Action on Hearing Loss Scotland, formerly the Royal National Institute for Deaf People, was another charity supported.

Sometimes the line between disability and disease can be blurred. The Brittle Bone Society and Alcohol Focus Scotland perhaps illustrate what I mean. With the increasing prevalence of dementia, it was essential to support Alzheimer Scotland, who firmly believe that no one should be called upon to cope with that awful problem alone.

The Smile Train UK is a charity that is so worthwhile. When children are born with a hare lip or a cleft palate, they are not only ugly but they have difficulty eating and breathing. An operation to correct these deformities must be carried out as soon as possible, and the Smile Train UK arranges this. Having seen many before and after photographs, I know how beneficial it is.

A charity I got so pleasantly involved with is the South Lanarkshire Wheelchair Curling Club. I had not heard of this club before but I greatly admired the members. I was so delighted to be able to support their competitions abroad. I got a Christmas card from them, showing some of them in their wheelchairs, all looking so cheery. I was thrilled to get this card, though it nearly reduced me to tears. I was also invited to their Christmas lunch and, while I would have loved to join them, it was just not possible. You cannot help but marvel at such courage.

Children's Charities

There are, of course, a great many children's charities and, sadly, it was possible to support regularly only a comparative few. Barnardo's was an obvious choice, as was the National Society for the Prevention of Cruelty to Children (NSPCC Scotland). The MacRobert Arts Centre in the University of Stirling provides creative learning and participation programmes for disadvantaged children and I deemed it worthy of a donation. An appeal came in from the Dream Team in Thundersley in Essex from someone who called herself the 'Dream Facilitator'! (How lovely to be one, I thought.) This charity enabled terminally ill children to fulfil some special longing that could perhaps not be easily afforded by their families. It gave me great satisfaction to be able to help them out a bit.

Animal Charities

There are also a great many animal charities, all doing splendid work. Having attended a fascinating demonstration in Stirling by Canine Partners, I became very interested in them. The dogs - mostly retrievers and labradors - are trained in the most amazing ways to assist disabled people and wheelchair users. They pick up things that have been dropped, bring articles of clothing to the disabled person, load and unload washing machines and press buttons at pedestrian crossings - to mention just a few of their skills. One of the wheelchair users said that before she got a dog she was more or less invisible but with the dog beside her she suddenly became noticed as a person again. I feel very enthusiastic about Canine Partners and they are one of the many charities I continue to support myself.

Pathfinder Dogs and Guide Dogs for the Blind are two other worthwhile charities training dogs to assist disabled people. We all know, of course, that not every dog is suitable for such training, so the final careful matching-up of a dog with a disabled person represents a great deal of effort and expense.

The Scottish Society for the Prevention of Cruelty to Animals (SSPCA) does a splendid job. Programmes on TV often highlight their work. I never cease to be amazed at the cruelty inflicted on defenceless animals. While it is heartbreaking to see the appalling conditions some animals are kept in, at least we know that everything possible will be done for them once they are rescued. It is sad to think that there is even a need for this charity, as people should not be behaving like that.

I've always been a great admirer of the People's Dispensary for Sick Animals. If you support the PDSA, you are not only helping animals who require veterinary treatment, but you are also helping people who may be finding it a struggle to find the money to pay for treatment for their much loved pets.

Katharine, the animal-lover

In N. Italy (Look who's on my lap!)   *With a darling dog in France*

A St Bernard in Switzerland   *A sloth with its baby in Cartagena*

The Trust also supported the building of the marvellous Small Animal Hospital in the Veterinary School of the University of Glasgow.

A little digression

I hope you will forgive me if I digress at this point as I wish to tell you that after Iain died, I thought I would like to have singing lessons. It may seem a strange thing to do in one's late seventies, but it turned out to be one of the best decisions I have ever made. I knew that Daisy Henderson, the soprano in George McIlwham's Trio Serenata, taught singing, so I contacted her and, after a half-hour assessment, I was taken on right away. Besides freelancing for Scottish Opera, Daisy performs as a soloist and also with different groups. She has also set up an agency for musicians called Classical Musicians Scotland. I often wonder if she realises the tremendous impact she has had on my life.

My weekly lessons, which are ongoing, opened up a whole new world to me and provided me with such interesting challenges. I learned a lot and am still learning. It has become a great hobby and I have now been through all the available publications with songs in French, German, Italian and Spanish. This interest of mine affected my charitable givings, so now back to the 'Charities Galore'.

Culture and the Arts

It was very satisfying to be able to support the National Theatre of Scotland and the Citizens' Theatre, Glasgow, for many years. I also became very involved in Pitlochry Festival Theatre, sponsoring three plays to date in memory of Iain, and taking a plaque on the memory wall. The National Trust for Scotland received an annual donation particularly for Arduaine Garden, south of Oban, where Maurice Wilkins, the former Head Gardener at Ross Priory, had gone to be in charge. The National Portrait Gallery was undergoing a very big restoration programme in 2010 and it was a pleasure to support it and later to view the completed job. The National Youth Orchestra of Scotland and Culture and Sport Glasgow also received donations.

In May 2012 I sponsored, through the Trust, the panel entitled 'Tam O'Shanter' of the Great Tapestry of Scotland and I later gave contributions to help with their plans for a permanent home in the Scottish Borders.

Scottish Opera was also supported over many years for all sorts of different things such as their Fiftieth Anniversary Appeal or their Emerging Artists. In 2013 and 2014 the Theatre Royal in Glasgow was undergoing a very major refurbishment by Scottish Opera and I was so glad to be able to support that. The transformation was fantastic and it was a very real pleasure and privilege to be present at the official opening. Latterly I was also able to help Opera Bohemia, a new company with young performers.

In 2013 I was keen to give money to the Royal Scottish National Orchestra New Home Appeal. This is now in full use and is a marvellous facility beside the Royal Concert Hall in Glasgow.

The Order of St John

As Iain and I were both in the Order of St John (mentioned elsewhere), we supported it ourselves and through the Trust with annual donations to the Priory in Edinburgh, to St John Glasgow (of which we were originally members) and to St John Dunbartonshire after our move to Gartocharn. Needless to say, I still support the Order enthusiastically.

For people in need

Well, there are plenty of them, aren't there? Freedom from Torture is a charity that distresses me a great deal, as their reports are inevitably so upsetting. I cannot understand how human beings can behave as they do towards other human beings but this appalling behaviour just goes on and on.

A charity I am particularly keen on is The Shipwrecked Fishermen and Mariners' Royal Benevolent Society based in Chichester, West Sussex. It does a fantastic job helping people who have fallen on hard times through no fault of their own. I love their Christmas cards and they sensibly send out their catalogue very early. The Chief Executive is charming.

East Renfrewshire Good Causes was set up in 2007 by Russell Macmillan, a registered blind man, and a few trusted friends, following his double pancreas and kidney transplant, to say thanks to God for his second chance of life. This charity does a remarkable job, helping people in a very practical way, often with domestic improvements and aids. Full details are given to supporters every so often, so they know exactly what their money is doing. It is always a most impressive report.

Combat Stress
This charity deserves a sub-heading to itself. I have been involved with Combat Stress for a very long time. It was originally the Ex-Services Mental Welfare Society and it now specialises in helping ex-servicemen who are suffering from Post Traumatic Stress Disorder (PTSD) and there are thousands of them. Their headquarters are at Tyrwhitt House in Leatherhead, Surrey, and their Scottish Headquarters are at Hollybush House near Ayr.

There were many fundraising events on offer, some of which - like the lectures in Edinburgh - I managed to go to. However, I very much enjoyed their events in London too, although there was a considerable effort on my part involved in attending them. I would go down by train, stay overnight at a club that had reciprocal arrangements with the Western Club in Glasgow, and attend the Annual Dinner which was held in a different gorgeous venue each year. I was usually seated beside generals, which I loved. Another delightful event was the Carol Service in the Chapel of Chelsea Hospital followed by a Reception in the Great Hall. On such occasions the Sloane Club was a very handy place for an overnight stay.

In 2007 I got an invitation to a dinner in Windsor Castle, hosted by our patron, HRH Prince Charles. The dinner was to mark the twenty-fifth anniversary of the Falklands War and it was a very clever idea because the event raised a huge sum of money for Combat Stress. I decided that this was unmissable so I flew to Heathrow, where I was met by a taxi, which took me to my hotel in Windsor the day before the dinner. Interestingly, the hotel had been the home of Sir Christopher Wren, the famous architect, and it still had Wren memorabilia in it. I explored Windsor and had a look at Eton College, but only from the outside. Next morning I joined the numerous members of the public, who were going to see the Castle, and I saw preparations being made for the dinner, of course. Although I was easily within walking distance of the Castle, the right thing to do was to take a taxi to the dinner and to have one booked for later. Security was tight and no one could possibly have been admitted without the relevant documents.

The drinks reception was held in a huge room and the then Chief Executive, Commodore Toby Elliott OBE, presented me to Prince Charles, saying that I was one of only three people from Scotland. Most of the guests were from the south of England, which was only to be expected, I suppose. I had no idea at the time that photographs were being taken, but I have two lovely photographs of myself with Prince Charles and also one with the Duchess of Cornwall. I was pleased to be able to speak to her and wish her every happiness in her recent marriage. She was very friendly and easy to talk to and I told her that she had been getting a very good press in a TV film I had seen recently and this interested her greatly.

Being presented to HRH Prince Charles at the Combat Stress Dinner in Windsor Castle. The then Chief Executive, Commodore Toby Elliot OBE, is on the right.

We then moved into the vast banqueting hall for the dinner. The tables were circular with huge silver tureens of flowers in the middle. On my left was Prince Charles's bodyguard and on my right, was a very charming gentleman. I told him I thought I knew him but I could not think why and he said it would be because of the TV.

Chatting to the Duchess of Cornwall in Windsor Castle.

It was Frank Thornton of 'Are You Being Served?' and 'Last of the Summer Wine'. His charming wife was also at the table but was obscured by the massive vase of flowers! The meal was really quite simple with a cold starter, followed by chicken, fruit trifle and coffee. Prince Charles gave a very appropriate speech - quite short - in which he expressed his concern for the plight of so many ex-servicemen.

After the meal, we were invited to make our way outside to the huge courtyard where the Band of the Royal Marines and the Precision Drill Squadron of the Royal Air Force entertained us. Fireworks lit up the sky of a pleasant summer evening. I was standing beside Prince Charles's driver, who - in response to my question - said that the Royals were going straight back to Clarence House. After they left, I had a very long wait for my taxi for the short journey to my hotel - and so to bed. Next day it was home to auld claes and parritch.

Although I am no longer able to go to the London events, I myself still support Combat Stress. I had a surprise letter from Mr Robert Marsh, a most charming person with whom I had had dealings in the past. He told me that after a gap of four years, he was so happy to be back with Combat Stress as their Director of Fundraising. We corresponded and he said he would like to see me as he was planning a trip to Scotland. The visit was duly arranged and we had an hour or so together, reminiscing over afternoon tea in my house. It was such a pleasure to see him again and we keep in touch. If you are dealing with a charity, what a difference it makes to have some personal contact.

Charities to do with Religion

The Salvation Army, for whom I have always had the highest regard, was a regular recipient of funds from the Trust; as was Glasgow City Mission, which I have visited several times. I never cease to marvel at the work done there. Opportunities exist for learning all sorts of things such as art, computing, cookery and much more. These skills also help to restore a sense of worth and achievement to the participants. Mission Aviation Fellowship, which provides planes to fly to inaccessible places, thus providing an essential lifeline to the outside world, is so worthwhile. Scottish Crusaders and the Boys' Brigade in Paisley were both supported and I was particularly happy to be able to 'rescue' the Whithorn Trust which was facing closure. Whithorn was the cradle of Christianity associated with St Ninian. I was also keen to support my former church in Netherlee and my present church in Helensburgh as it embarked on a highly ambitious plan for much-needed new halls, which are now in use.

Iain's special interests

As a former pupil of the High School of Glasgow, Iain had become a very generous benefactor, so I became one too. Having 'lost' my own school, I very much enjoy having an input here. Because of Iain's interest in boats, the Maid of the Loch Appeal and *The Waverley* were both given money. A very interesting and unusual charity was REMAP (Scotland), which had been set up by Iain's friend, Robbie Bowie, who was a brilliant engineer. REMAP (Scotland) devises special mechanical aids to assist people with unusual disabilities and I was always keen to support it.

My special interests

The University of Glasgow has always been dear to my heart and there is always plenty to give to there. There is the Chancellor's Fund, if you wish the University to use the money as it thinks fit, but you can, of course, indicate exactly where you would like the money to go. Over the years the Trust supported the Small Animal Hospital in the Veterinary School and the James Herriot Scholarship Fund special appeal. The University's Research Facility, south of Rowardennan on Loch Lomond, received donations from the Trust. This was SCENE - the Scottish Centre for Ecology and the Natural Environment - which I visited more than once. The Trust also supported the exciting plans for the new campus development on the site of the former Western Infirmary. I have seen the plans and they are fantastic and will transform that part of Glasgow.

I have also supported, through the Trust, the University of Strathclyde, where I worked for sixteen years and, in particular, the major refurbishment of the organ in Barony Hall.

Through the University of Edinburgh's Department of English Literature, the Trust supported the new Edinburgh Edition of the works of Robert Louis Stevenson (thirty-nine volumes).

Though I have never been a geographer, the Trust and I have supported the Royal Scottish Geographical Society, based in Perth, which I think is a most worthy recipient of funds. I keep up my membership.

Many years ago Iain and I got involved in the Wurlitzer Organ Concerts in Clydebank Town Hall. Unfortunately, the organ suffered serious damage due to flooding in the basement, where it was kept, and a new home had to be found for it. It is now established in Pollokshaws Burgh Hall. The Wurlitzer is a highly technical beast and requires a great deal of skilled attention, which it gets from a superb, dedicated team - the Scottish Cinema Organ Trust (SCOT). It has been a pleasure and a privilege to support SCOT through the Trust and also by myself. Throughout the year highly gifted performers are engaged for concerts on the only working cinema organ in Scotland.

Miscellaneous Charities
The following do not seem to fit into any of the above sections: Cosgrove Care; the Caledonian Railway at Brechin; St Conan's Kirk (an A-listed beautiful church on Loch Awe in need of repair, a building much loved by Iain and me); the Museum of Scottish Lighthouses (Fraserburgh); and the Wildfowl and Wetlands Trust, Caerlaverock Wetland Centre, Dumfries-shire, for the Sir Peter Scott Observatory Project.

***

This has been a long chapter. It represents the hard and constant work of ten years of my life. It has been a great privilege to be able to help. I hope that Iain would have been pleased with my efforts. In 2015 the Stockbroker and the Trust Manager both felt that the Trust should be closed down, due to my age. I was in complete agreement as this decision enabled me to disburse the funds as I wished and no one was going to be left with an unwelcome responsibility.

The lovely Christmas card I got from the marvellous South Lanarkshire Wheelchair Curling Club. (Good luck to them!)

21 - Epilogue

'I will not wind a lang conclusion' (Robert Burns)

In October 2015, I received a letter from the Priory of St John in Edinburgh to intimate my promotion in the Order from Commander (2008) to Dame. What an amazing surprise and great honour!

After my acceptance, I heard eventually that the Investiture would be in the Canongate Kirk in the Royal Mile in Edinburgh on 16th March 2016. This was, of course, much easier for me than going to London. When the great day came, everyone involved was delighted and relieved that the weather was dry. I was fortunate in getting a lift from 'St John' friends in Drymen, three miles away, and we picked up the former Chancellor, John Ford, in Balfron. We arrived at the Church at 1.30pm. Although the ceremony did not start till 3.30pm, there were already several people there and we had to be there early in any case.

There were only six postulants - four gentlemen were being invested as Knights (including the Lord Lyon King of Arms) and myself and Fiona Crighton, the then Receiver-General, as Dames. About 3pm we were led down the central aisle to our seats in the front row. At 3.30pm a trumpet fanfare announced the arrival of the procession of forty-eight persons from St John's House further up the Royal Mile. I was delighted to recognise both trumpeters! Since Major General Mark Strudwick CBE, KStJ, was being admitted as our new Prior, there were other Priors there too and the ten banners in the procession made it a very colourful sight.

The Investiture was conducted by HRH The Duke of Gloucester GCStJ, our Grand Prior, who made it abundantly clear that he was conducting the Investiture on behalf of HM The Queen. The six postulants were invested early in the ceremony, after which the Duke of Gloucester publicly thanked our immediate past Prior, Lieutenant Colonel Sir Walter Hugh Malcolm Ross GCVO, OBE, KStJ, for the successful completion of his term of office.

Then followed the Installation of Major General Mark Jeremy Strudwick CBE, KStJ, as our new Prior of Scotland in a very formal but impressive ceremony ending with a proclamation given by the Lord Lyon King of Arms. After a hymn, the Gospel reading and address by the Dean, the Very Rev Dr John Cairns KCVO, CStJ, and another hymn, the ceremony drew to a close with the National Anthem. As the organ voluntary was played, the procession left the church first, with the new Knights and Dames following on.

A coach took us to the Palace of Holyroodhouse at the foot of the Royal Mile for the private reception, but first a large photograph was taken of those in the procession, with the Duke of Gloucester seated in the middle. At the reception it was a pleasure to see so many friends and acquaintances. I left with my friends about 6.15pm and finally got home at 8.20pm. What an amazing privilege to be part of such an awe-inspiring ceremony! It was indeed a day to remember.

Confucius said, *'It does not matter how slowly you go, as long as you do not stop'*. I am taking that to heart. If there were to be an epitaph - and there will definitely not be one - it should read simply:

HIC JACET
KATHARINE MARGARET ELLA LISTON
She did what she could.

Acknowledgements

First of all, I must thank Dr John Cairney for sentencing me to a year's hard labour.

I owe a huge debt of gratitude to Daisy Henderson for typing the manuscript and making useful comments.

Many thanks are due to Bill Kean for the photograph of the baby on the cover. The photograph of the Investiture on the cover was taken by Donald Sinclair Photography – Edinburgh.

I would also like to thank The South Lanarkshire Curling Club for allowing me so graciously to reproduce their Christmas card.

But most of all, I cannot express strongly enough the thanks and appreciation due to my publisher, Paul Murdoch, who steered me through the publication process so ably and put up with my fussy ways with such good grace.

KMEL

For more publications by
NEETAH BOOKS
please visit
www.neetahbooks.com

Lightning Source UK Ltd.
Milton Keynes UK
UKOW07f0320240117
292745UK00012B/54/P